A Layman's Commentary

Volume 3

Books
of
Wisdom

**Job, Psalms, Proverbs, Ecclesiastes,
Song of Songs**

John Devine M Eng Sc

BALBOA.
PRESS
A DIVISION OF HAY HOUSE

Scriptures taken from the Holy Bible, New International Version®, NIV®.
Copyright © 1973, 1978, 1984, 2011 by Biblica, Inc.™ Used by permission of Zondervan.
All rights reserved worldwide. www.zondervan.com
The "NIV" and "New International Version" are trademarks registered
in the United States Patent and Trademark Office by Biblica, Inc.™
All rights reserved.

Balboa Press books may be ordered through booksellers or by contacting:

Balboa Press
A Division of Hay House
1663 Liberty Drive
Bloomington, IN 47403
www.balboapress.com.au
1-(877) 407-4847

ISBN: 978-1-4525-1299-0 (sc)
ISBN: 978-1-4525-1300-3 (e)

Printed in the United States of America

Balboa Press rev. date: 02/11/2014

CONTENTS

The Books of Wisdom

These five Books of the Old Testament make up a volume of literature in poetic form that addresses most of the issues of life.

They explore and give advice on the existence of evil and reasons for suffering and how to deal with these matters.

They include a collection of songs of prayer, petition, praise and worship that enrich our personal relationship with God.

They provide wise observations and practical knowledge on universal moral order with guidelines for a meaningful and joyful life.

They explore the frustrations and ultimate futility of life without God.

There is an expression of love between a king and a country bride which can be applied to one's relationship with God.

They describe the creative and sustaining power of God at work in the universe and in the human being.

They outline God's purpose and plan for mankind and the futility of existence without it.

Job

Introduction – The Book of Job was written in the finest poetry and addresses the question of all generations and cultures – **why do the godly suffer?** It traces the story of a good man who fell from prosperity to poverty in possessions, family and health. He was put on trial to test his faithfulness to God in every situation and he passed the test. Through it all he learned valuable lessons that are equally applicable in the modern day. Job was counseled by friends who did not understand his situation. God eventually answered Job and restored him to a position of prosperity. Job was recognized by Ezekiel Ezk 14:14,20 and James Jas 5:11.

Author – Unknown. Could it have been Elihu?

Period – The lifestyle of Job was similar to that of Abraham and the patriarchs around 1800 BC.

The theology is monotheistic and consistent with other Old Testament experience down to 1000 BC.

Job lived in the land of Uz in the Syrian desert 1:1.

Uz was the firstborn son of Nahor, brother of Abraham Gen 22:21 - also 10:23.

Theme – God is active in the creation and involved in the everyday affairs of mankind. He is sovereign and working out his eternal plan Rev 10:7.

There is a reason for everything There is purpose behind every event and experience – even in suffering. We learn much from the discourse of Job with his friends in the testing of his faith. God speaks to us through Job's experience.

Job asked questions of God and sought answers – he wanted a reason for suffering. Like Thomas, who wanted physical proof of the resurrection before he would believe, Job asked on our behalf, so we can learn from the answers Jn 20:24-29.

His friends, though God-fearing men gave clinical advice, much of which contained truth, but was not relevant.

A closer walk with God Job learned that it was not the moral order that had broken down – it was his understanding of the depth and wisdom of the sovereignty of God. Through this encounter he came into a closer, more intimate relationship with God.

The spiritual realm We come to see something of the spiritual conflict in which we are involved Eph 6:10-13. The discussion in the heavenly realm described in 1:6-12 and 2:1-7 must have been revealed by God to Job after his experience 42:10.

Overview

Job presented eight discourses as he searched for an understanding of his suffering.

His three friends responded with their advice followed by comments from a young colleague.

Eliphaz – Knowledge and worldly views without discernment expressed in self-righteous judgment – was an evil source involved there? 4:12-16.

Bildad – Traditional wisdom presented in philosophical platitudes – he thought that well-being depends on works.

Zophar – Common sense in its most brutal application - Job's suffering must have been the result of sin Jn 9:2.

Job – The teachings he had been reared on and lived by failed him. His greater suffering was not from his losses and afflictions but because his experience did not agree with the theories he had embraced. The moral foundations of his world were being challenged.

Elihu – Wisdom of a learned young man with lack of real experience – while his advice is sound he adds nothing to the matter of Job's suffering.

God's answer to Job -

- The three friends were ignored
- No answer was given on how to understand or avoid suffering – no new light on God's moral principles and purposes
- Job was challenged to match God's power, understanding and wisdom in creation. He humbly submitted to God and was restored to a deeper relationship
- Wellbeing comes from recognition and worship of the Creator Ps 8:1-9; 19:1-14
- The case against the devil as the promoter of evil and the continual accuser of the righteous was proven
- The three wise men were rebuked for their self-righteousness, lack of understanding and impatience with the sufferer.

SUMMARY
Job on Trial - The First Test 1:1-22
Job on Trial - The Second Test 2:1-13
Job's First Discourse - Suffering is real and may be expressed in grief 3:1-26
Job's Second Discourse – Faithful through Trials 6:1 to 8:22
Job's Third Discourse – Need for a Savoir to remove God's rod 9:1 to 11:20
Job's Fourth Discourse – The Sovereign God, Almighty 12:1 to 15:35
Job's Fifth Discourse – My Witness, Advocate, Intercessor is in heaven 16:1 to 18:21
Job's Sixth Discourse – My Redeemer lives and so will I 19:1 to 20:29
Job's Seventh Discourse – Willful arrogance of independent mankind 21:1 to 22:30
Job's Eighth Discourse – Testing brings forth gold 23:1 to 25:6
Job's Ninth Discourse – The fear of the Lord – that is wisdom 26:1 to 31:40
Elihu's Contribution – The Awesome Grandeur of God 32:1 to 37:24
The LORD answered Job – Out of the storm 38:1 to 42:6
Lessons to be learned 42:7-16

Job on Trial - The First Test

1:1-5 **Introduction** Job was a person of exemplary character. His respect for God permeated his life. He had integrity and status and he petitioned God on behalf of his children.

Job's blameless life did not exclude him from testing – in fact it was because of his faithfulness that attention was drawn to his character v8 -

• we must recognize that there is purpose in all our trials 2Cor 12:7-10 – we may not understand the events at the time but will know the reward of faith in the end Heb 11:8-10

• we persevere knowing that in our victories we will receive the crown of glory that will never fade away 1Pet 5:4,10.

1:6,7 **The Heavenly Realms** Here we have insight into the ongoing activities of the spiritual world Eph 6:12 -

• God is sovereign and controls all the activities of the universe

• Satan is not an imaginary being - he is the adversary, the accuser of the brethren Mt 4:1-11; Rev 12:10

- He is subject to God in all that he does – he can only operate to the limits of God's restraint 1Cor 10:13
- He is continually at work in the lives of mankind for harm and to promote evil 1Pet 5:8 – particularly in the lives of those who deny God Eph 2:1-3.

1:8 **God drew attention to Job** God had confidence in Job and knew that he could trust him to remain faithful in spite of everything he would encounter. God knew Job would be able to stand this trial. Job was being honored by God. We can see that the trials we undergo are an opportunity for us to honor God by our steadfast faith. This information must also have been revealed to Job in his restoration to fellowship with God 42:10.

1:9-11 **Faith must be tested** Satan gave little attention to Job because of his faith – as we resist him he will flee from us Mt 4:1-11; Jas 4:7. He found excuse for Job's faith and suggested it was because of God's blessing but if blessing was withheld Job's faith would fail. This shows why our faith must be tested - *in order to prove it is genuine 1Pet 1:7;* Heb 11:6.

1:12 God gave permission for the trial - within set limits. We see that the circumstances of life are within the control of our Heavenly Father Mt 6:31-34.

1:13-22 The extent of Satan's vindictiveness is revealed – he has no interest in our wellbeing - only in using mankind as a means of challenging the authority of God. We know that God is not vindictive Lam 3:31-33.

We cannot understand the fate of Job's family.

Despite such loss Job acknowledged the sovereignty of God and worshiped in humility v20,21. Real worship comes from acknowledging who God is – not because of what we receive, or our situations. This too, must be tested - *give thanks in all circumstances 1Thes 5:16-19.*

In all this he did not sin by charging God with wrongdoing v22.

Job on Trial - The Second Test

2:1-10 On the next summons Satan chose not to refer to the continuing faithfulness of Job. We must see here that it is really the evil one who is on trial!

Again God drew attention to Job – *he maintains his integrity v3.* Satan's response was to claim that physical health was the reason for faith. God gave permission for Job's health to be taken - again within set limits. We

can see another reason why the righteous suffer – *that your faith - may result in praise, glory and honor when Jesus Christ is revealed 1Pet 1:7.* Job even lost the support of his wife. She could not understand the testing or the faith!
Shall we accept good from God and not trouble! v10.

Three Friends Came to Console

2:11-13 Colleagues came with genuine sympathy to comfort Job. They brought wise words which relate to the general understanding of suffering and evil as expressed by many throughout the generations and commonly held today. However they were not applicable in this case as we know from the spiritual battle over Job's faith in the heavenly realm. Advice and counseling require discernment with compassion and empathy.

There was silence for seven days – showing the magnitude of his suffering.

Job's First Discourse - Suffering is real and may be expressed in grief

3:1-24 **Questioning God** Finally Job broke the silence. He did not understand his situation and so he questioned God. It is good to know that we can bring our feeling, problems and suffering openly before God where consolation, understanding and strength will be found Ps 73:16,17. Sometimes our complaints are ahead of God's purpose 42:10.

Many of our questions can't be answered in this life v20.

3:25,26 **Peace and rest** Anxiety and fear produce real problems in our lives – the things we fear often materialize v25. Anxiety and fear develop stress and reduce our effectiveness. Yet they produce nothing productive. We must learn to appropriate the words of Jesus – 'be anxious about nothing!' Mt 6:25. Faith means that, having done all we can to plan, we can rest in the knowledge that God is in control Mt 11:28-30.

4:1-11 **Eliphaz' Response** Job's character was confirmed. However his situation must be due to having done wrong – a commonly held opinion v7. While there are inevitable consequences for wrongdoing each situation may involve several factors and result in a number of positive outcomes.

4:12-21 **Fear and dread** Was this a demonic dream to persecute and discourage Job? Or was it just the negative thoughts of human ideas? The devil would have us live in fear of pending judgment v12-16 - *blessed is he whose transgressions are forgiven, whose sins are covered Ps 32:1.*

5:1-27 Job was accused of foolishness and should call on God for the testing to stop! Job was being corrected and should ask for mercy v17. Developing a daily relationship with God through Jesus provides guidance on the right course of actions to take.

Job's Second Discourse – Faithful through Trials

6:1-10 Even in desperation Job was faithful and did not deny God's Word v10. Believing in God's absolute character and the truth of his eternal promises provides security in our daily lives.

6:11-13 When everything was taken from him he realized his own inadequacy – and his need for God.

6:14-30 Now that he felt helpless he found no consolation in wisdom that did not apply to him v21. He was aware that his integrity was at stake and sought encouragement v29.

7:1-16 Job could not understand the intensity of his suffering and longed for relief even thinking of the possibility of suicide v15,16. Negative thoughts produce negative actions – positive thoughts provide answers Nu 13:28-33. At times like this we need to focus on God, his Word and his promises Ps 40:1-3.

7:17-21 He pondered the importance of man to God and the need for the testing of faith v17. He recognized that God was targeting him and appealed for forgiveness of past sin v21. We know that God loves us and has forgiven our sins when we come to faith in Jesus Rom 5:8.

8:1-22 **Bildad's Response** Job's suffering was blamed on wrongdoing – if he looked to God and did upright deeds he would be restored. This is easy theology when things are going well. In times of difficulty we need to be reminded of God's promises – we need encouragement and strength to persevere.

Job's Third Discourse – Need for a Savoir to Remove God's Rod

9:1-13 **The Mighty God** Job acknowledged the truth of what was said but knew it did not apply in his case. He declared his knowledge of the wonder of the unknowable God - who made the constellations. These wonders of the cosmos are arguably today the best known examples of a constellation (Ursua Major, the **Bear**), a nebula **(Orion)** and a star cluster **(Pleiades)** v9; 38:31,32. The motivation for science is that we may be able to discover the *wonders that cannot be fathomed v10.*

9:14-35 **The Righteous God** Job knew that good works cannot make a person righteous before the absolute and holy God v15; Eph 2:8,9. Justice must be served – wickedness must be punished with the rod of God's retribution. He could not dispute with God and foresaw the need for a savior, advocate, intercessor who could remove the judgment of sin from us v32,33. God provided his Son Jesus Christ who fulfilled all of these tasks.

10:1-3 Job could not dispute with God but continued to bring his situation to God in humility v2. The great blessing of prayer - we can talk with our Father, express our thoughts and desires and expect an answer to our needs.

10:4-7 **Do you see as mortal sees?** Some may think that God is unfair when viewed from our mortal perspective. The wonder is that Jesus took on flesh - was born as a babe - that he could experience our sorrows and provide our needs - so that we might experience eternal life Heb 2:14-18.

10:8-22 **You gave me life** We received all we have from God, life, ability, relationships, location and duration – we are shaped and moulded, given understanding. But he watches over our spirit and requires that we be answerable for our actions and endeavors – for good and bad v13-15.

11:1-20 **Zophar's Response** Again Job's suffering was attributed to wrongdoing. Some of the statements are correct. However when we see God's denunciation of the three advisors we understand how wrong many of our ideas about suffering are! 42:7-9. We cannot fathom the mysteries of God – his thoughts and ways are higher than ours v7; Is 55:8,9.

Job's Fourth Discourse – The Sovereign God, Almighty

12:1-9 The condemnation of Job's friends was heave on him. Yet even as he suffered the answer to his prayer came with understanding v4. There is purpose in everything that happens on earth v9.

12:10-25 *In his hand is the life of every creature and the breath of all mankind v10.* All wisdom, power, counsel and understanding are his v13. He controls the elements and all those in authority v 15-24. We do well to acknowledge this as we will be called to account for our stewardship Lk 12:35-48.

13:1-28 **Desire to speak to the Almighty** Job longed to stand before God and discuss his case instead of with human counsel v3. He did not know the position of those who now *have confidence to enter the Most Holy Place by the blood of Jesus Heb 10:19*. Still his devotion to God was unwavering – he had confidence that his future was in God's hand. This is the evidence of real faith that no matter what may befall we will hope in God – *though he slay me, yet will I hope in him v15;* Rom 4:3,18.

14:1-14 **Will he live again?** Job expressed the common belief of the Old Testament era that death was the end of existence v14. This is also the conclusion and resignation of natural science and the philosophies of the world.

14:14-22 **I will wait for my renewal to come** Yet within him he had a sense that there was more to life than death v15. This desire is deep within every human being - *God has also set eternity in the hearts of men Ecc 3:11.* The resurrection of Jesus is the only confidence we can have that there is life after death.

15:1-35 **Eliphaz' Response** Wise in the commonly held view that suffering and loss are the result of wickedness he did not understand the deep reason behind Job's situation or the extent of God's grace.

Job's Fifth Discourse – My Witness, Advocate, Intercessor is in heaven

16:1-22 **My Advocate on high** Job would have encouraged one confronted with suffering, not accused them. But as he contemplated the depth of his situation he gained revelation into the glory of God. He considered the justice and goodness of God and the frailty of mankind. As he did he caught a glimpse of the Advocate v19-21 – the one who speaks to the Father in our defense - Jesus Christ the Righteous One – he is the atoning sacrifice for our sins 1Jn 2:1,2. This was all arranged before the creation of the world! 1Pet 1:20.

17:1-16 Despite his despair Job held to his integrity and his hope in God – *the righteous will hold to their ways and those with clean hands will grow stronger v9.*

18:1-21 **Bildad's Response** The self-righteous platitudes of one who does not share the problem. The companions were in the process of missing the point of Job's experience. While they saw his suffering as being the consequence of wrong things he must have done they did not understand that trials always have a deeper purpose.

Job's Sixth Discourse – My Redeemer Lives and So Will I

19:1-29 In the midst of meditation deeper revelation came! From the depth of his innermost being the Holy Spirit drew assurance of the plan and purpose of the Almighty.

• *I know that my Redeemer lives and that in the end he will stand upon the earth* – this prophetic insight was revealed to the Apostle John about the end time Rev 14:1

• *And after my skin has been destroyed yet in my flesh I will see God v25-27.* Job foresaw the resurrection perhaps 1,800 years before the resurrection of Jesus Christ. His prophetic words mirror the teachings of Jesus and the apostles Jn 11:25,26; 1Cor 15:42,49; Phil 3:21; 1Jn 3:2. This resurrection is the expectation of all believers based on the assurance of Jesus Jn 11:25,26.

• *How my heart yearns within me v27* Job expressed the cry of all believers – *Even so, Lord Jesus come! Rev 22:20.*

20:1-29 Zophar's Response He talked of the short lived gains of the wicked and the ultimate end of their ways inferring that this was the case with Job. Understanding of the deep things of life regarding trials and testing of faith had still not come to the advisers as they continued to condemn him.

Job's Seventh Discourse – Willful Arrogance of Independent Mankind

21:1-34 The problem of evil Job still had unanswerable questions – 'why do the wicked prosper – when they ignore God?' This issue is considered by most people.

They say to God 'Leave us alone! We have no desire to know your ways.' v14. People want to cast off restraint Ps 2:1-3. Without God there is no absolute standard of morality or responsibility – right and wrong become a matter of consensus.

The great sin of the individual is to disregard God in willful ignorance and arrogance – *the fool says in his heart 'There is no God' Ps 14:1.*

Job recognized that wisdom and prosperity are in the hand of God for he judges the highest v22. We may not understand why one prospers and another fails v23-26. We know that - *in his heart a man plans his course, but the LORD determines his steps Pro 16:9.*

22:1-30 Eliphaz' Response The common view expressed by Elphaz is incorrect - that God is not concerned with our conduct. God does delight in those who seek him – *who hunger and thirst after righteousness Mt 5:1-16.* His delight was in Job 1:8. It was because of his faith and trust that God brought Job to be tested – not for his wickedness.

Submit to God and be at peace with him – accept instruction from his mouth and lay up his words in your heart v21,22. This is the path to be followed by every believer in a personal daily relationship - but it does not necessarily ensure worldly prosperity. We can find delight in the Almighty in all circumstances and he will lift up your face Ps 63:1-8; 3:3-5.

Job's Eighth Discourse – Testing Brings Forth Gold

23:1-11 **If only I knew where to find him** In his suffering Job had begun to think that God had forgotten him. This is a common feeling. We know that this is never the case Mt 10:30.

Job searched for a deeper relationship with God – this was part of the reason for his situation. He wanted to know more of God's presence. Compare his search here with the experience of David v8-10; Ps 139:7-10. Job knew he was being tested and that he would come through as a better person – as gold v10. When we understand that this is the reason for the trials of life we and develop perseverance and the right attitude Jas 1:2-4; 5:11.

23:12 I have treasured the words of his mouth more than my daily bread It was because of Job's love for God's Word that he could stand the test – he read it, knew it, believed it, treasured it and applied it. In fact his faithfulness to God's Word led him to a higher level of experience of God's purposes. When we learn to apply daily the spiritual disciplines of prayer, reading the Word, worship, fellowship and witnessing we will grow in our knowledge of God and our relationship with him! We will also be *thoroughly equipped for every good work 2Tim 15-17.*

23:13-17 **Devotion to God and His Word** This will lead us to an awesome reverence of God that will keep us through the dark times and empower us in his service Hab 2:20.

24:1-25 **The subject of evil was raised again** Our personal desire for justice comes from God and must be reflected in our daily lives in the way we act towards others v1.

We see from the audiences in the heavenly realms that there is a constant battle between good and bad, between right and wrong for the souls of mankind 1:6,7; 2:1,2. This conflict will reach culmination in the last days Rev 13:14-17.

It seems at times as if God does not administer justice v12.

Suffering and injustice must be viewed in the light of the cross – God required Jesus to suffer for our sin – *God made him who had no sin to be sin for us, so that in him we might become the righteousness of God 2Cor 5:21.* We must give ourselves to alleviate suffering, injustice and poverty in the world. God's justice will come and it will be swift and final v22; Rev 20:12-15.

25:1-6 **Bildad's Response** Despite the belief that suffering was due to wrongdoing the view was expressed that righteousness and purity for mankind are unattainable. This is confirmed by our recognition that 'no one is perfect'. We recognize that there is an absolute standard of righteousness which we do not attain. We need a means by which our wrongdoing can be forgiven and our acceptance by a righteous God can be secured. Righteousness can only be received from God - *through faith in Jesus Christ to all who believe Rom 3:22.*

Job's Ninth Discourse – Fear of the Lord, that is Wisdom

26:1-14 **Trust in God** There is a degree of satire and frustration in the comments of Job as he finds no help in the counsel of his friends. He focused again on what he knew of the greatness of God in creating and sustaining the earth. That the earth is suspended over nothing is an amazing observation for his time v7 because the source and nature of the four energy forces that uphold the universe including gravity are still not understood Col 1:17; Heb 11:3. Job recognized that his knowledge of God was but on the outer fringe of God's works.

27:1-6 **Job declared again his commitment to God** – *as long as I have life within me, the breath of God in my nostrils, my lips will not speak wickedness v3,4.* A positive profession of faith is the path to victory in every situation Phil 4:4-9; 1Thes 5:16-19. It is humbling to think that every breath is God's!

27:7-23 **The fate of the unbeliever** The majesty and absolute holiness of God demand that justice will be administered. This is fundamental to the inherent standard of all people. The love and mercy of God have provided a remedy for this judgment – *he who has the Son has life 1Jn 5:11,12;* Ezk 18:23; 2Pet 3:9.

28:1-28 **Wisdom** Man's quest for gold and silver is relentless. But Job's desire was for something more precious - more wisdom to understand God's ways. He declared that God alone knows the path to wisdom as he is its source v23. *The fear of the Lord - that is wisdom and to shun evil is understanding v28.*

29:1-25 **Search Me O God** Job's meditation had led him to examine his past and his deep motives. Self-righteousness and pride in his own efforts began to surface and were recognized. It is through suffering and meditation with God and his Word that we begin to see the real nature of our character and are exposed to the sanctifying power and refining work of the Holy Spirit Ps 139:1,23,24; Gal 5:22-26.

30:1-31 **Genuine Humility** Job's suffering and trial made him see his conceit and arrogance in his own self-importance. He was stripped of all that made him confident in his own dignity v15. He reviewed his past actions and thoughts for he had sought to live a blameless life and found no reason for his plight.

31:1-40 He continued his resume of good deeds which he believed should have kept him from suffering. Then he ran out of words! Rom 3:20-23. *Blessed are the poor in spirit, for theirs is the kingdom of heaven Mt 5:3.*

Elihu's Contribution 32:1 to 37:24

32:1-5 **God is justified** This young man who had observed the discussion pointed out that while Job had sought to justify himself his friends had failed to help him with his dilemma and so he was compelled to comment v1-5.

32:6-22 **The Spirit within me compels me** Wisdom does not only come through age and experience. The fear of the LORD is the beginning of wisdom and good understanding Ps 111:10.
But it is the Spirit in a man, the breath of the Almighty that gives him wisdom v8,18. As we read God's Word and apply it in our lives we grow in knowledge and effectiveness.

33:1-33 **The Need for a Redeemer** We must begin our search for wisdom by acknowledging God - *the Spirit of God has made me; the breath of the Almighty gives me life v4.* While Job maintained his integrity before God, pride led him to suggest that God was treating him unjustly v8-10.
God speaks in many ways – in dreams, visions, words, suffering, chastening and correction v12-22. We all recognize guilt and are aware of our wrongdoing and sin v27; Ecc 7:20; Rom 3:23.
I have found a ransom for him There is need for One to pay the debt, for a Redeemer v24,28; Gal 3:14.
Through prayer we find favor with God and joy at seeing his face v26. He gives us strength to persevere and delivers us v28.

34:1-37 In all of these statements Elihu continued to reveal reverent truth about the nature and character of God -
• *Far be it from God to do evil, from the Almighty to do wrong v10* – this axiom brings security or resistance.
• Always know that God is just! *It is unthinkable that God would do wrong, that the Almighty would pervert justice v12*
• **If God were to withdraw** *his Spirit and breath all mankind would return to dust v14-15* The atoms that make each person and every other

physical object in the universe were produced in the first stars from the same particles created in the early moments of the universe – we are dust from the stars Gen 3:19

• **Breath of God** v14 The only plausible source of the energy from which matter and everything else came including the four energy forces that hold us together is the eternal God Heb 11:3

• *His eyes are on the ways of men; he sees their every step v21* This is great encouragement to those who love God Ps 139:1-10

• *He is over man and nation alike v29* This is the reason for our confidence as we pray for leaders and world events

• **We cannot come to God on our own terms** We must accept his self-revelation in his Word, acknowledge our sin, repent and accept his grace v33.

35:1-16 **The awesome nature of God** does not diminish his concern for mankind. God is grieved by sin v6 so much so that he sent his Son to remove the offense of our sin Rom 3:23-25. He does delight when people turn from their wickedness and repent Lk 15:7,10. He wants us to pursue righteousness and holiness because that is his nature Mt 5:48.

36:1-21 **His eye is no us** God is concerned for mankind and firm in his purpose v5. He does not take his eyes off the righteous because they have a glorious future v7. Obedience and service do bring his blessing v11. God will strengthen those who suffer and deliver those who are afflicted v15.

36:22-33 **Our confidence** Our focus must always be on the greatness of God rather than our circumstances, to extol and to praise him rather than to complain about our situation v22-25. His Person and his works are beyond our understanding v26. The phases of the water cycle through evaporation (from the seas), condensation (as clouds), precipitation (as rain) recirculation to be accumulated in the seas – this hydrological cycle essential to life was not known at the time of writing – the ultimate driving force is still not understood v27-30; Amos 5:8.

37:1-24 **My heart pounds** To be excited about God's presence is great blessing v1. *The joy of the LORD is your strength Neh 8:10.* We should frequently stop and consider his wonders v14. A close relationship with God will carry us through all situations v23,24. This is possible through Jesus Christ 1Jn 1:3.

The words of Elihu were a fitting prelude to God's answer to Job.

THE LORD ANSWERED JOB – Out of the Storm The word 'LORD' means 'YHWH', the eternal personal name of God. It relates to the Covenant relationship between God and mankind Gen 2:4; 3:8. This name is used of God in the counsel of the heavens in 1:6-12 and 2:1-7. It is also now used in chapters 38 to 42 where the LORD speaks with Job. The word 'God' used by Job and his associates in the remainder of the record is the more general term which identifies the Creator, monotheistic, self-revealing One who is also the 'Almighty' sovereign all powerful One Gen 1:1. The use of these names here is in conformity with the rest of Scripture. Job's philosophical discussions generally referred to God in the third person, as distant, impersonal and unresponsive. While this is the attitude of many today, Job was to learn that a deeper, personal relationship is possible with the LORD 42:1-6.

38:1-38 **The Grandeur of God's Creation** The LORD revealed himself in his awesome presence with words that humble all mankind. The creation is his work, the revealed evidence of his glory and power. No one can answer the question put to Job *'Where were you when I laid the earth's foundation?' v4* – only the arrogant can challenge it.

There is no viable explanation outside of God for the beginning of the earth or the universe. Over one hundred questions were asked of Job that continue to challenge the greatest human minds - science can observe, define and measure but cannot explain why or cause to happen. The wonder of these issues being raised over 3,000 years ago is that they are still beyond our grasp today!

- *the earth's foundations* required a unique, narrow, finely balanced life zone involving diameters, masses, distances, angles, eccentricities, rotational and orbital speeds of earth, moon and sun to maintain the atmosphere, temperature, chemistry and water for the existence of life on earth v4
- *on what were its* (**the earth's**) *footings set* – energy holds the motion of the earth relative to the sun v6,7 – it is suspended over nothing 26:7
- *shut up the sea behind doors* – the earth has a bulge at the equator of 1 in 297 due to its rotation - if not the seas would rise towards the equator and flood the land v8; 2Pet 3:3-7
- *given orders to the morning or shown the dawn its place* – the varying orbit and rotation of the earth provide day, night and the seasons v12
- we have only begun to discover diversity at *the depths of the sea v16*

- no man has ever *comprehended the vast expanses of the earth* let alone the universe v18
- *the abode of light* - the source of all energy which occurred instantaneously at the beginning of the universe is still outside our understanding v19 - *what is seen was not made out of what was visible Heb 11:3.* The Bible explains that this energy came from God – from his Word – *by faith we understand that the universe was formed at God's command Heb 11:3.* Where is the abode of light? Only since the 1920's has science fathomed the answer to this question. When the first and most fundamental element of matter (hydrogen) was formed from pure energy at the beginning of the creation some 1% of its mass was stored. That additional mass is currently being released progressively over the life of the sun to provide light and heat on earth – as well as human life.
- *where does darkness reside* – darkness has no substance, it is the absence of light (energy) – it has no residence v19
- *the storehouses of the snow* – the molecules of water vapor crystallize to form an infinite variety of hexagonal shaped snowflakes displaying incredible diversity and beauty, for the storage of water! v22
- *where the lightning is dispersed* – from interaction of wind (energy) and moisture droplets – stripped electrons gravitate to the bottom of clouds where they are stored and discharge to earth or other clouds v24
- *control of the environment* – who brings the wind, rain, dew, frost and ice to provide grass and who withholds it v24-30; the force of the wind and measure of the waters 28:24-27; the balance of wind, water and water vapor by weight in the life-sustaining water cycle 36:27-29
- **water is essential for life** – the earth and human body consist three quarters water, the universal solvent that moderates the climate on earth v22-30
- we cannot influence *the constellations in their seasons* let alone **bind, loose or bring them forth** v31,32. Pleiades is now known to be an open star cluster (how to bind it?) and Orion is tightly bound (how to loose it?)!
- *lead out the Bear with its cubs v32* - Ursa Major, the Bear, is known to move at the head of the seven main stars (cubs) that make up the Great Bear 9:9
- *the laws of the heavens* are still basically beyond our reach both in understanding and control v33 – the trajectory of three bodies can't be defined

- *who endowed the heart with wisdom v36* – the transition from inert matter to life, atom to self-replication – is not known. There is expectation (hope?) that spontaneous generation may be discovered as a law of physics
- *who gave understanding to the mind v36* - the basis for self-awareness and intellect is still unknown – the interface between physical and mental, brain and consciousness, instinct and morality Gen 1:26; 2:7
- **God is Spirit** – there is also the perception of the spiritual; denied by the materialist and reality to the believer 1Cor 2:11-16
- **Spirit talks with spirit** It is of interest to note that the LORD does not address the wonder of the human body Ps 139:13-16. He confronts Job as 'made in God's image'. This is Spirit conversing with spirit! Nu 12:3,8; Ps 42:7,8; Jn 4:23,24.

The LORD who speaks v1 Such an encounter with God as this is not conceivable for one choosing only to accept the formation of 'self' from a single lifeless atom over billions of years through a mindless progression of cells, fish and animals by a myriad of small adjustments totally by chance and for no purpose or reason and destined for extinction.

Yet for the believer made in the 'image of God' and redeemed by the Son of God such revelation is humbling, exhilarating, motivational, purposeful and assuring of eternal destiny.

38:39 to 39:30 The Origin of Life Having reviewed the wonder of the physical universe the LORD turned to animal life – the lion, raven, goat, deer, donkey, ox, ostrich, peacock, stork, horse, grasshopper, hawk and eagle – all understood and provided for by the Almighty. Not a sparrow will fall to the ground apart from the will of your Father Mt 10:29-33.

Physical science and evolution do not exclude the creative power and Presence of God. In fact, the fine-tuning of over twenty seven cosmological constants in order to form and maintain life, which were present at the first moment of existence demands that Someone set the parameters.

40:1-5 Job's Response – in abject obeisance and submission
The LORD gave Job the chance to question God's power, purpose and justice. This opportunity will be given to every human being when every knee will bow and every tongue confess at the judgment Phil 2:9-11; Rev 20:12-15. All those who have encountered the revealed Presence of God have fallen face down in reverence and humility - Moses Ex 3:4,5; Isaiah Is 6:1-7; Ezekiel Ezk 1:26-28; John Rev 1:17. This is to be expected before the eternal Creator and Sustainer of the universe Is 66:1,2.

The LORD Continued

40:6-14 **The High and Lofty One** The LORD continued to confirm his sovereign power and moral order Is 57:15. Job's pride and self-righteousness were directly challenged v10; 32:1. We cannot stand in our own righteousness before the living God or expect to save ourselves v14; Eph 2:8,9.

40:15 **Created after their kind** Job was reminded of the animals *which I made along with you v15*. This confirmed the Genesis account that God made all things according to their kind – vegetation, creatures, animals Gen 1:11,21,25 all after their kind Gen 6:20. And finally God created mankind – unique, intelligent, moral, responsible and accountable Gen 1:26,27; 1Cor 15:38-41.

40:15-24 **Behemoth - land dweller** Further evidence of God's creative diversity was given in describing two examples chosen for their impressive form. The greatest of creatures, the behemoth, a land dweller v19 and leviathan, a sea creature 41:1 may refer to the hippopotamus or elephant or the crocodile or whale but their descriptions fit more with prehistoric creatures! The uncertainty of their nature confirms the limited knowledge of man and the all-knowing wisdom of God.

41:1-34 **Leviathan - sea dweller** The detail with which these two monsters are described challenges the mind and reinforces the knowledge and sovereignty of God. We can only imagine their fearsome might v33,34.

No one is able to stand before or against the LORD – everything under heaven belongs to him v10,11. His creative power and providence contrast with the insignificance, limited ability and finite knowledge of man.

The Outcome

42:1-3 **Knowledge of God** Job already knew that the LORD could do all things and that his eternal plans cannot be thwarted 12:14. But it was an impersonal understanding 3:25. As a result of this encounter his knowledge of God was enlarged.

We must be open to fresh revelation as we grow in our search for meaning to life. Rather than squeeze God into our mould, a god made in our own image that answers to our expectations and whims (or does not answer) we must be prepared to expand our mind to fathom the glory of the infinite, eternal Creator. For those who have limited themselves to a physical world the god of their imagination is questionable. But those who have been opened to the revelation of the LORD are continually developing in their knowledge and experience of the spiritual, eternal reality.

***42:4-6* Relationship with God** Job now experienced the direct revelation of God and bowed down in awe in his Presence – *my ears had heard of you but now my eyes have seen you v5*. Before he had knowledge of God - now he had encountered, had seen and understood. He entered into a personal relationship with God. His perspective of God and himself was changed. Self-importance and pride were destroyed and he repented of them in dust and ashes v6.

We may have knowledge of God but we need to have a personal heart experience in his Presence that will impact our thoughts, habits and the way we live. This encounter is available to all who will seek it Jer 29:11-14; 1Jn 1:1-4; 5:11,12 When pride and self-interest submit to God in repentance we are able to live in his Presence Mic 6:8. Seek him with all your heart 1Chr 29:11-13.

LESSONS TO BE LEARNED

There are things to learn from Job's encounter with the LORD –

• God acts according to a principle too great and exalted for his actions and motives to be fully grasped and understood by the human mind Is 55:8,9. We must see our situation in relation to the awesome greatness of God's Person and plan, humbly admitting our lack of knowledge.

• Character must be developed through adversity. Athletes come under discipline not for punishment but for the contest and to win the prize Heb12:1-4. They undergo training and correction to improve their skill and effectiveness 1Cor 9:24-27. Such effort develops perseverance and leads to maturity Jas 1:2-4; 5:11. Spiritual growth depends on coming closer to God through Jesus Christ 2Tim 2:15.

• Faith requires that our actions move us beyond the realm of physical proof Heb 11:6. So faith must be put on trial as in the case of Job that it may be proved genuine 1Pet 1:6-9. Abraham also was tested to demonstrate his faith Gen 22:1,2,12. All who are commended before God are recognized because of their faith Rom 1:17; 3:21,22; Heb 11:2.

• Did Job realize how much depended on his faithfulness and continued trust in God? Do we recognize that we too will be put in situations that will require us to be faithful? It is only gold that is worth putting in the fire! 2Tim 2:20,21.

- We must also see suffering in the light of the cross. Jesus the most righteous suffered the most and for the sake of others - us! Often we are required to suffer for Christ and for others 2Tim 3:12; 1Pet 2:21-25. All suffering will be vindicated at the Second Coming.
- That Job emerged victorious demonstrates that God's grace and provision are able to cause us to stand in any godly trial 1Cor 10:13; Phil 4:19.
- God's revelation of himself as eternal Creator and sustainer of all things exposes the great sin of arrogance in denying him and his provision. Natural science and evolution do not exclude the presence of God or his moral order. Rather the mystery of the source of energy and the frailty of human nature demand an eternal, holy Creator.
- Worship of God is the response to all circumstances of life -
In his hand is the life of every creature
And the breath of all mankind 12:10.

In Conclusion

42:7-16 The statements about suffering made by the three advisers were acknowledged as not applying to Job – they did not take into account the deep things of God.

God referred to Job as 'my servant' because he stood the testing of his faith.

God was vindicated for his confidence in Job who maintained his faith throughout the whole trial 2:10; 6:10; 27:3-6. In addition Job's pride and self-righteous attitude was replaced by humility and a greater understanding of God's Person.

The trouble the LORD had brought upon him v11 confirms that there are many things outside our understanding but all things are under the control and sovereignty of God – *we know that in all things God works together for the good of those who love him Rom 8:28.*

Job was restored after his trial.

The Problem of Suffering

Some aspects to be considered –

1. God is almighty, sovereign over all creation, holy, righteous and just – the Absolute perfect good Ex 34:5-7.

2. The world was created as good, without fault, innocent and with eternal perspective Gen 1:31.

3. God did not create evil or suffering. Evil is refusal to do good - as darkness is absence of light, absolute cold is the absence of energy, so evil is the consequence of rejecting good Jas 1:17,18.

4. Evil came into human affairs because of the disobedience of mankind Gen 3:6. Much preventable evil and suffering occurs because of the rebellious human nature – conflict, self-centeredness, coveting, domination, deserted spouses and children, breaking the Ten Commandments Jas 4:1-4.

5. Human freewill involves responsibility and accountability, requiring the testing of faith and developing of character – we choose between right and wrong Jas 1:2-4,12.

6. There are consequences as a result of going against God's laws including suffering Deu 28:1-68.

7. Bad things happen as warnings or discipline, as stated by the prophets of Israel Is 1:2-20; 45:7; 54:16. God is not vindictive. There is purpose in every event Lam 3:33; 2Cor 12:9.

8. There is a spiritual dimension and evil is present Eph 2:2,3. There is a battle for the souls of mankind. Evil must be resisted and overcome 1Pet 5:8,9. Job's suffering was due to the vindictiveness of the evil one Job 1:9-11; 2:4,5.

9. God entered into our suffering to overcome evil by the death of his Son, remove the consequence of sin and provide eternal life to the believer Jn 3:16. He gives power to overcome evil and suffering in our lives 2Cor 4:16-18; 1Pet 1:6-9.

10. In all things God works for the good of those who love him Jer 29:10-13; Rom 8:28; Eph 2;10

11. We would all like a perfect world now, with no evil, suffering or pain. If evil were removed and evildoers punished it would mean the loss of choice – we would no longer be in the image of God, no longer human and no longer able to enter into special relationship with God Rom 3:3-18,23; Heb 2:5-8.

12. We look forward to a world for those who have chosen to acknowledge the Creator and follow his ways, with no evil, suffering or pain – this is the promise of God Rev 21:3-5.

Psalms – Book of Praises

Introduction – The Psalms are unique in human history.
God is the central focus. They are rich in spiritual intensity, expressing worship of God – the cry of the ordinary person to the Almighty. Some confront God and obtain a response. They are intimate conversations between God and his people - expressions of the heart – joy, worship, happiness, frustration, despair and penitence.

They cover most life experiences They provide a plan, a pattern to follow and they have application for us today. The simple rhythm, style, imagery, pattern, pairs of lines, echoing thoughts, repeats and opposites easily translate into other languages. They were often accompanied by instruments.

Authors and Period – The Book of Psalms was compiled over centuries for common use by congregations at the Temple services. The Book as we know it including all the titles and notes were in the Hebrew manuscripts when translated into the Greek 'Septuagint (LXX)' Old Testament around 250 BC.

Songs of praise have been recorded by Israel from long before David. Moses composed a psalm at the time of the Exodus around 1446 BC Ex 15:1-21 and Psalm 90. Deborah and Hannah composed psalms Jud 5; 1Sam 2.

Nearly half the 150 psalms are attributed to David (73) - Ps 2–41; 51–71; 108–110 and 138–145. Fourteen relate to events in David's life - Ps 3, 7, 18, 30, 34, 51, 52, 54, 56, 57, 59, 60, 63 and 142. Some were his personal prayers which later became formal worship. Other authors were Temple musicians, choir leaders and officials 1Chro 25:1 – Asaph (12), sons of Korah (10), Heman and Ethan, also Moses and Solomon while 50 are anonymous.

David ruled from 1010 to 970 BC. The Exile began with the fall of Jerusalem in 586 BC – Ps 74:3,7,8; 79:1 and 137. The Return from captivity occurred around 538 BC – Ps 126.

Special Features – The impact of David's life was enormous. He was known as Israel's singer of songs 2Sam 23:1 and composed other psalms 2Sam 1:17; 22:1; 23:1; 1Chr 16:7. He was the one whom 'the Lord sought out as a man after his own heart' as a ten year old boy 1Sam 13:14.

David raised the level of human experience in his encounter with God using such words as exalt, exult, extol, magnify, up raise, awesome, glory, majesty, splendour, shout aloud for joy, greatly rejoice, yearn, pour out, cry out, faint. He brought unity to Israel and focus on God with great blessing. His own heart and vivid personal relationship with God together with the turmoil of his life set the style and formed the nucleus of the worship of the nation of Israel.

The Psalms are consistent with the teaching of the New Testament and serve as a wonderful example and encouragement for us today.

The Psalms are in five groups – Ps 1–41; Ps 42-72; Ps 73–89; Ps 90-106; Ps 107–150. There is no clear reason for this division, perhaps location, occasion, season or choir preference.

Themes – Communication between God and Mankind. There are a number of possible subject divisions –

• **Worship** The purpose of existence is to glorify the Creator and enjoy him forever. The awesome God who alone inhabits eternity created the universe with human beings at the pinnacle in order that mankind might worship him and commune with him for eternity. The Scriptures begin with mankind in communion with God and end with God dwelling in relationship with mankind forever Gen 3:8; Rev 21:3.

Worship is based on who God is rather than on what he has just done. It involves reverence, awe, adoration and honor. There is within the nature of the individual the capacity to obtain great benefit from the worship of God Ecc 3:11.

• **High Praise** A major focus in the Psalms is the exuberant praise of our Great God. Praise is seen as the natural and constant response of the individual to the wonder, majesty and goodness of God both for who his is and for what he has done. Praise is shown to be the path into God's Presence even from the depths of sorrow. Praise is a source of joy and wellbeing to the one who participates. Praise is also seen to be a conscious decision of the mind and will.

• **Laments** Some psalms come out of a feeling of despair and injustice. They describe the suffering of life brought about by personal circumstances or persecution by others with a call for deliverance. Some deal with individual sin, confession and repentance. Most of these laments end in praise as they lead away from the situation and come to focus on God.

• **Thanksgiving** A constant thread of the Psalms is the attitude of thankfulness to God for all he has done and especially for his act of choosing us as his own. It is also the response to the experience of being born again and the promise of eternal life.

• **Remembrance** We are called to remember who God is and what he has done in the past – to remember all his goodness. This reminds us of his faithfulness and provision, his power and purpose, his promises and his Presence.

• **Wisdom** Psalms address the deep issues of life and give advice for the wise. They extol the importance and benefits of delighting in and living by God's Word and describe the consequences for those who have no time for God.

• **Kingship** The Sovereignty of God over Israel and all mankind is declared. He is also sovereign over all circumstances. His ultimate rule over all is predicted.

• **Confidence** Faith, hope and trust in God are expressed as the foundation for facing every situation. We are assured that God will never leave us. This inspires commitment and acknowledges dependence. The Psalms hold nothing back from God who sees all thoughts, words and actions – love, joy, happiness, grief, anger and frustration flow out. This is possible because God cares for us as a Father cares for his children and such openness leads to close relationship with him.

• **Vengeance** Some Psalms speak of retribution (they are imprecatory). It is difficult for us to reconcile these thoughts with the New Testament. We must first understand the ultimate vindication of the righteousness of God against all evil 149:6-9.

The conditions of the times must also be taken into account.

We embrace the model of Jesus which shows the true nature and character of God and the attitude required of man. The ultimate demonstration of God's character is seen in the life and example of Jesus Christ and his selfless sacrifice for us on the cross of Calvary Mt 5:1-16; 2Cor 8:9; Phil 2:5-11.

• **Relationship with God** There is personal encounter with God who is at the centre of the psalm as man reaches out to him 95:6,7. There is direct access and intimate relationship with God 89:15-17; 100:1-5. David had an awareness of the Presence of the Holy Spirit and he knew the joy of salvation 51:11,12.

The Word of God is seen to be the guideline for that encounter with God 18:30; 19:7-14; 119:89.

- **Revelation of the Character of God** The Presence of God is real and dynamic 27:4; 63:1-8; 73:23-28. He is the Almighty who created and sustains all things – who knows all, sees all, has all power 139:1-24. All things are subject to him – the creation reveals his glory 8:1; 19:1-4. He is good, wise, righteous, all faithful, holy, kind, merciful, forgiving 36:5-9; 89:14; 145:17. He dwells with the humble and contrite who seek him and put their trust in him 37:3-11. He resists the proud and self-centred who have no time for him and will bring them to nothing 10:4. He is the Sovereign LORD who will ultimately come to rule the nations in righteousness and peace, judge the world and put down all wickedness and injustice 9:7,8; 50:4-6; 96:11-13.

These truths develop our understanding and experience of God.

- **A Pattern to Follow** A pattern of life is presented which is relevant for today. This leads us in our relationship with God and the way in which we deal with everyday situations 33:1-5; 34:1-10. We learn how to praise God and live a life of thanksgiving in his Presence 37:23,24. We learn to trust, hope and depend on God 40:1-3. The practice of calling on him through prayer for guidance and direction is also emphasised. We learn about petition, confession and repentance 5:1-7; 51:1-17.

- **Attitude** The Psalms reveal the attitude of David in his approach to God and life. He acknowledged God in all situations, giving praise and thanks, inquiring and seeking guidance, making God the main focus of his life. The application of these principles is revealed in the attitude of God towards David – *the LORD gave David victory everywhere he went 1Chro 18:6.* This may be contrasted with the materialist who lives in a physical world with no acknowledgement or awareness of God.

- **Prophecies of the Christ (Messiah, Anointed One)** The Psalms speak of David as God's anointed king. However many statements go beyond the life and experiences of David. They look forward in time to a ruler from God who will put all things right. They have fulfilment in Jesus Christ. David prefigures Jesus as the servant of God who is the Great King over all the earth 10:16; 24:10; 47:1-9; 145:1-13; Lk 24:44.

All things in creation work to the order of God's plan and purpose 33:10-15. He chose Israel as his people to reveal him to the world and Jerusalem (Zion) as his city 87:1-3. He chose David as the anointed king and made a covenant to establish David's throne forever 89:3-4, 20-29,33-37.

Psalms look forward to the coming of a new Anointed King and Priest of the line of David who will set up God's kingdom forever 89:26-29;

110:1-7. He is God's Son who will be the perfect King and will rule all nations in peace, justice and righteousness 2:2-9; 22:27-31; 29:10,11; 45:6; 72:18,19.

The fact that Jesus used the Psalms confirmed the veracity of these documents – that they are historical, that they are the eternal Word of God and that they were being fulfilled by him – *everything must be fulfilled that is written about me in the Law of Moses, the Prophets and the Psalms Lk 24:25-27; 44-47.*

This is particularly remarkable in the prayers and in the experience of the cross 22:1-31; 69:9.

There are at least twenty one Messianic Psalms – that speak about Jesus or that he fulfilled. These psalms predict his incarnation, suffering, death, burial, resurrection, ascension, exaltation, and ultimate rule (ref p66). The Holy Spirit inspired this prophetic revelation which is confirmed in the Book of Acts and the Epistles Acts 2:24-36; Eph 4:7,8; Heb 1:5-13; 2:6-8; 5:5-10; 1Pet 2:4-10. The authors of the Psalms were identified as having the prophetic gift 1Chro 25:1; Acts 2:29-31.

It is possible to personalize the Psalms – in so doing we make them our own and appropriate the blessings for today. It will only come through application.

PSALM 1 – Delight in the Word of God

The first psalm defines the way of life for the believer and the means of maintaining that life. The alternative is also described. This model is consistent throughout the Bible Jn 15:7; Heb 4:12,13; 2Tim 3:16.

v1 **Blessed** – a state of well being, in all circumstances. O the joy of such a person! Who does not walk / stand / sit – in the way of the world – a progressive trend.

v2 **His delight is in the WORD** – he meditates on it day and night Jos 1:8. The Law of the LORD, 'torah', means teaching or instruction and included the Scripture of the day.

v3 The fruit comes! He prospers! Jer 17:8,9; Mt 13:18-23.

v4-6 The LORD watches over his way – he is in right standing with God.

PSALM 2 – The LORD and His Anointed

The second psalm prophetically describes the sovereignty of God and the coming of his Son, Jesus to judge the nations and to rule on earth in the end time Dan 4:17; 7:9-14; Rev 19:15.

v1,2 **The World is against God and His Anointed** There will be centralised world government and ideology, a build up of resistance and worldly philosophy until the end Rev 17:13,14.

v3 **Mankind resists the authority of God –**

• they cast off restraint, to be independent, free from restrictions, authority and responsibility – 'self' becomes the centre of their world Pro 29:18; Act 4:25-28

• they rebel against God, denying or ignoring God's existence

• they reject his Law and perfect way of life Mt 11:28-31

v4 The ultimate authority is the LORD over all.

v5,6 The King – the Son, will judge the nations, on earth, out of Zion, despite the rebellion Rev 20:12.

v7 **Jesus is declared the Son of God** Mt 3:16,17; Heb 1:5.

v8 The nations of the whole earth will serve the King of kings and LORD of lords 110:1; Mt 24:30; 28:18-20.

v9 **The millennium rule of Jesus** will be with an iron sceptre when God's Law will be applied 45:6; Rev 12:5; 19:16.

v10-12 **A warning to the kings and people of earth** - the LORD is loving, merciful, forgiving and to be feared. Choose to serve, fear, worship and rejoice in him while the day of salvation is here – for his wrath will flare up in a moment Rev 22:12.

PSALM 3 – My Glory and the Lifter of My Head

Written by David when he withdrew from his son, Absalom who sought to take over the kingdom 2Sam 15:13,14. It is the first of many psalms which describe the path out of despair to victory.

v1,2 How many do we think are against us.

v3,4 Speak confidence before the LORD – declare who I am in Christ Jesus! Eph 1:3.

Who is my **'Glory'**? Who is the centre of my affection – the lifter of my head? I must determine this and declare it!

v5-8 **Sweet Sleep** - the promise of God comes to those who put their trust in him and learn to walk with him Ps 4:8; 127:1,2; Pr 3:24. Meditate with the LORD on your bed 63:6. If you go to sleep with the LORD you will wake up in his Presence 139:18.

v8 How can we expect blessing if we ignore God? Commit your way to the LORD - your plans will succeed Pr 16:3.

Selah – a common phrase encouraging us to pause - and reflect about the truth expressed!

PSALM 4 – Assent to Victory and Peace
David began in despair and rose to greater joy and sleep in peace by remembering the promises of God.

v1,2 Answer me! How long! We may express our feelings to the LORD. He hears, knows and feels them anyway.

v3 I KNOW – speak **words of faith** – the LORD does hear and act. Confess what we know of his promises.

v4 Do not let anger separate me from you. I search my heart and respond. I can lie in anxiety and recycle my fears - or I can focus my attention on you.

v5,6 I speak confidence in you and look to you - your face shines on me! (Anthropomorphism – ascribing human features to God).

v7 The outcome of my devotion and meditation in your presence is greater joy - to the full Is 12:2,3.

v8 Praise and worship leads to sweet sleep, peace and security 3:5-8; Col 3:15-17.

PSALM 5 – In the Morning – I Will Seek You!
The practice of prayer and communication with God daily leads to gladness and joy – particularly when we start the day.

v1,2 Prayer includes praise, worship, asking – with sighs, a cry for help.

v3 I will begin each day in your presence. Then I will wait in expectation. This is the walk of trust and faith, the path to joy.

v4-7 I WILL come into your House, I WILL bow down in reverence - by your great mercy – not in my own strength. Prayer is a matter of the will – a decision of the soul.

v8-10 Lead me, O LORD – in your righteousness - make straight my way – keep me from the way of the world Mt 6:13.

v11,12 I will be glad as I take refuge in you – I will ever sing for joy - for you are like a shield.

PSALM 6 – You Accept My Prayer
v1-3 Make your plead to God, in anguish, in all kinds of problems. Discipline is never in wrath but in love Heb 12:11.

v4-7 Because of your unfailing love – the basis for my request.

v8-10 I can speak in confidence – you hear and you accept my prayer! Mt 7:7-11; 1Jn 5:14,15.

PSALM 7 – Cry for Justice

There was personal enmity between some of the members of Saul's tribe of Benjamin and David 2Sam 16:5; 20:1.

v1,2 I take refuge in you – O LORD my God! I can bring my concerns and hurts and leave them with you rather than being consumed by bitterness and thoughts of retaliation.

v3-8 If I have done evil…..! Judge me by my righteousness, my integrity! While I hunger and thirst after your righteousness I thank you for the righteousness that comes by faith in Jesus, from first to last Mt 5:6; Rom 1:17; 3:21,22.

v9-13 O righteous God – you search my mind and heart!

v14-16 Evil thoughts produce evil actions and disappointment. Evil deeds always return with consequence.

v17 I give thanks and sing praise to your Name because of your righteousness, O LORD Most High.

PSALM 8 – The Glorious Plan of Creation

We must each answer for our response to the natural revelation of God in the creation Rom 1:20.

v1-6 How majestic are you LORD!

- You made the creation and set your glory over it
- You made mankind and set us as rulers over all things v5
- You will bring all things together under Christ as the Head – this is the mystery of creation v6 Eph 1:9,10.

v2 **Praise -** the weapon you have ordained to silence the devil, through Jesus, on the lips of your children Mt 21:16; Eph 5:18-20; IThes 5:16-19 – we must use it !

v3 **The wonder of Creation** – the work of your hand. We need to consider it! If we do, you will reveal yourself.

You have revealed your Presence, so men are without excuse.

v4-8 To contemplate the glory of God reveals the importance of mankind that God should care about us. Man is so insignificant by comparison yet –

- You care for him, made him a little lower that the angels v5
- You crowned him with glory and honor v5; Heb 2:5-9
- You made him ruler over all you created v6

- Angels, as ministering spirits, serve him Heb 1:14
- the world to come will be subject to him Phil 2;9-11
- everything will be under his feet 1Cor 15:27!

Jesus is the forerunner and confirmation of all these truths Heb 2:6-13; 1Cor 15:20,23.

v9 O LORD, our LORD, **how majestic is your Name in all the earth!** We must each look at the creation in wonder and awe – how much greater it is to exalt in the One who created it!

PSALM 9 – The Basis for Praise

v1-6 I will praise you, with all my heart. I will tell of your wonders, I will be glad and rejoice.

Praise is a matter of the will – not feelings or circumstances.

Man looks from the physical side, from under the circumstances.

Faith sees from God's perspective – for we sit in the heavenly realms with Christ! Eph 2:6.

v7,8 The eternal reign of the LORD is coming in judgement, righteousness and justice – look ahead Jn 14:1-4; 16:8.

v9-10 You are my refuge and stronghold. I am never forsaken because I always seek you.

v11-18 I profess with confidence what I know of you, O LORD, in my prayers, my praise and in my daily life.

PSALM 10 – Stand on the Promises of God

v1 There are times when the LORD appears to stand far off – to hide from me. I feel abandoned.

v2-11 The original sin manifests in pride, self-sufficiency, arrogance, no room for God v4.

v12-15 You do see – you consider – you do help me v14.

v16-18 Ultimate justice belongs to you. I must always stand on the promises of God - reminding myself of who I know you to be and what you have promised in your Word v17.

PSALM 11 – Finding Peace in Panic

v1 I must turn to the LORD, always, as my first choice.

v2,3 Especially when I cannot do anything about it.

v4 The LORD is in absolute control of everything. I can come to you – into your presence. I need to come to you more often and wait on you, even in the good times.

v5 You test my faith by the circumstances of life to develop my character. You see, you examine everything that happens - you are omnipresent.
v6 Vengeance belongs to the LORD Deu 32:35. I must leave room for your wrath Rom 12:19-21. My care for the wicked may lead to their salvation.
v7 I will see your face when I seek you Jer 29:11-13.

PSALM 12 – Godly Compared with the Ungodly

v1-4,8 The feeling of being alone. Of being amongst mankind without restraint – a fearful thought.
v5-8 The LORD acts on behalf of the weak and needy in accordance with his flawless Word and protects me.

PSALM 13 – I Will Trust - The Energy of Faith

The trials of life confront us every day – the joy of the LORD is our strength Neh 8:9,10.
v1-4 The cry of despair, wrestling with my thoughts.
v5,6 Trust, rejoice, sing, on the basis of who you are O LORD and what you have already done for me. The song of praise on the lips of the saint brings the joy of the LORD 22:3; 149:5.

PSALM 14 - The LORD Restores

The question of the Creator's existence is not a philosophical one – it is a matter of eternal destiny.
v1 The ultimate folly and great sin – to say there is no God.
It is not a matter of intellect but of independence.
v2,5,7 The LORD looks for those who understand, who seek him and is present with them.
v3,4 Mankind without restraint - human evil has no limit. Under certain circumstances human nature is unpredictable Rom 3:23.
v5,6 The LORD dwells with me! It is because of Jesus Rev 3:20.
v7 Pray for Israel, their day of salvation will come Rom 9:25-27.
Pray for the unsaved - O that salvation would come for them.

PSALM 15 – I Dwell in Your Sanctuary!

Each person has a moral conscience and a sense of perfection which are incompatible – requiring the need for a Savior.
v1 I have access to the presence of God, his dwelling! Heb 10:19,20. How often do I go in to exercise my privilege?
v2-5 Having been redeemed I have guidelines for life Mt 5:48.

v5 I will never be shaken!
Thank you, LORD Jesus, for bringing me into the Father's presence and causing me to walk in His ways.

PSALM 16 – Eternal Pleasures!
This psalm recognises the hope of eternal life - the choice between eternal life and conscious oblivion.
v1,2 You are 'My LORD and God' – I make a positive decision and declaration.
v3,4 I seek those who love and serve you, who delight in you. They strengthen me, as iron sharpens iron Pr 27:17.
v5-9 You gave me all I have – life, ability, location and relationships. It is you who determine the steps of my life Acts 17:24-28. Thank you, LORD for security, provision and counsel.
v7-9 I have set you always before me – I am glad and I rejoice.
v10 Jesus is my forerunner to eternal life. As he rose again, so will I Jn 11:25-27; 1Jn 3:2 – foreseen by David Acts 2:31.
v11 You have made known to me the way to eternal life - through faith in Jesus Christ. You fill me with joy in your presence – now and forever!

PSALM 17 – I Am the Apple of Your Eye!
v1-5 Vindicate me, probe my heart, examine and test me.
v6-14 I seek your guidance and follow it, so I dwell in the shadow of your wings – protected from evil v8.
v15 I am satisfied with seeing your face – when I wake up each morning. When you appear I will be like you 1Jn 3:12.

PSALM 18 – The LORD Delights in Me! 2Sam 2:1-4
David's prayer when delivered from Saul after thirteen years of flight and waiting for his anointing to be revealed 1Sam 20:1.
v1-3 I love you, my strength, fortress, I praise you and am saved.
v4-19 Near death, I cried to you and you heard from your temple v6, even the earth responded. You reached down from on high and took hold of me v16.
v20-29 You reward me as I commit my ways to you.
You keep my lamp burning and turn my darkness into light v28.
v30-50 **You Lead Me in Victory** Your way is perfect, your Word flawless. You are my strength; you make me strong and make my way perfect v32. You make my feet like a deer to stand and to run on the heights v33.

v35 **You stoop down to make me great** – a cause for my future confidence, trust and praise. You stooped down, LORD Jesus to provide my salvation, became a man and died on Calvary to take away my sin Phil 2:6,7 and give me eternal life Jn 3:16!

PSALM 19 – The Glory of God Revealed - to lead us to Him
The physical, moral and personal evidence of God.

v1-6 **Revealed in the heavens** – the physical sky and the earth – the work of your hands cannot be denied - except by those who choose foolishness 14:1.

v7-11 **Revealed in your Word** – you are perfect, trustworthy, right, radiant, pure, all together righteous, more precious than gold, sweeter than honey and my great reward.

v12,13 **Revealed in my heart** – as I personally sense your presence, correction and leading and commit to your way v12.

v14 May I be pleasing to you – at all times!

It is this evidence for the Presence of the Creator that requires each person to draw a conclusion – *since the creation of the world God's invisible qualities – his eternal power and divine nature – have been clearly seen, being understood from what has been make, so that men are without excuse Rom 1:20.*

PSALM 20 – Trust in the Name of the Lord
v1-5 A declaration of faith and confidence in your provision. Our plans committed into your hands prosper. We shout for joy as you lead us in victory 2Cor 2:14.

v6-8 Now I know that the LORD saves, he answers from heaven with his power – this is the starting point for my confidence.

PSALM 21 - Give Thanks for Past Blessings and Eternal Life
v1-5 The cause for future confidence and trust is what you have already done! I look back and give thanks.

v6,7 Surely you have granted me eternal blessings – in your presence. This is the aspiration of all mankind - life after death - made possible through the life, death and resurrection of Jesus Jn 1:11-13; 1Jn 5:11-13. This is the assurance given by Jesus Jn 11:25,26. There is no other hope Jn 14:6; Acts 4:12.

v8-12 At the LORD's appearing your people will be vindicated v9 – we will sing and praise your might v13.

PSALM 22 – The Psalm of the Cross

There are at least twenty-one Messianic Psalms and some forty with Messianic overtones (ref p66).

This Messianic Psalm foretells the coming of Jesus, the Christ, the Messiah, the Anointed One.

No incident in the life of David can begin to account for the experience expressed in this psalm. It describes in detail the suffering of crucifixion, not used until introduced by the Roman Empire around 150 BC -

• the sufferer's cry v1, no answer v2, humility, scorn, sense of rejection v6, mocking, insults v7, offensive derision v8

• bones out of joint v14, thirst v15, pierced hands and feet v16, bones exposed v17, dividing of garments v18

• praise in despair v3, called from eternity v10, no plea for vengeance, resignation to the fate of suffering v11

• recognition that none could rescue but God v11

• identification of the afflicted One – the Suffering Servant, forsaken for a time v24; Is 53:1-11; Mt 27:46

• the purpose is world vision – all will bow before him v27, he will rule over nations v28, final judgment of all people v29, world evangelism v22.

v3 **Enthroned on praise** You ride on (enjoy, inhabit, are enthroned on) the praise of your people, in worship and in service. We encounter the Presence of God, especially in the midst of praise and worship. On the cross Jesus demonstrated the highest praise in service to God.

v22-26 **I will proclaim your work** – the testimony and witness of the redeemed. You have done it - sins forgiven, salvation for the believer, through the suffering and death of Jesus.

v27-30 All people will kneel before him v29; Phil 2:9-11.

v31 **It is finished** - this was the cry of triumph by Jesus from the cross Jn 20:30. You have done it – Your work on earth and my eternal redemption!

God's plan of salvation for all mankind based on faith in Jesus Christ alone, as uniquely and consistently revealed throughout the Scriptures is described here in this psalm Rom 3:21,22.

PSALM 23 – The Lord – My Companion

From an early age David recognised that his relationship with God was that of the shepherd with his sheep.

v1 **You are my Shepherd** - everywhere I go you are there with me. The prime requirement for a sheep is to be in the Presence of the Shepherd Jn 10:14-16,27-29.

v2 You provide for me in all that I need - I will not want - like a sheep, I put my trust in you Mt 6:25-34.

v3 You keep me on the right path - as I walk with you.

v4 I will fear no evil, even in the midst of the worst situation, because you are there, with me Mt 6:25-34.

v5 When I am serving you - you provide, anoint me and cause my cup to overflow.

v6 Your love pursues me, everyday and I will dwell with you forever! The expectation of eternity confirmed by Jesus Jn 3:16.

PSALM 24 – Into Your Presence I Come!
Perhaps David sang this song as he brought the Ark into Jerusalem to be the centre of the people's lives 2Sam 6:1,2,17.

v1,2 **Everything belongs to you O LORD**. You created the world, and me to dwell in it. I lift up my soul - to you!

v3 **You are holy** – all who approach you will know Is 6:1-8.

While we now have access to your presence we must seek you with our whole heart, as a matter of will, in reverence and awe Heb 10:19; 12:28,29.

v4-6 **Examine your heart** – O seeker! Walk in his ways for they are good. We are vindicated by God our Savior.

v7 **I open the doors of my heart**. You came in! The Lord Almighty – the King of glory! Rev 3:20.

PSALM 25 – My Integrity and Uprightness
v1-3. A declaration of trust – I lift up my soul. It is a matter of the will. I make a decision each day to trust you.

v4-7. I request your guidance, all day long. I thank you for not remembering past rebellion and wrongs that you have forgiven.

v8-15. I commit to follow your ways. I confide in you as you confide in me v14. My eyes are ever on you v15.

v16-22. I turn to you for help in the midst of trouble because my hope is in you v21.

PSALM 26 – I Love the Place Where You Live

v1-7 A declaration of sincerity with nothing to hide. Test me, try me, examine me, for I would be more like you 2Cor 3:16-18.

v8-12 I love to be in your presence, O Lord, my feet on level ground v12. You are ever present, in my heart!

PSALM 27 – Your Face, LORD, I Will Seek Mt 5:6,8

v1-3 With you to guide and my eternal salvation assured, who shall I fear? In troubles, even then will I be confident.

v4-6 One thing I seek – to know your presence and gaze upon your beauty – to grow in my relationship with you.

v7-12 My heart tells me to seek your face and I do Jer 29:12,13.

v13 I am confident I will see your goodness, always.

v14 Wait for the LORD, be strong, take heart and wait Is 40:31.

PSALM 28 – I leap for Joy in Your Presence

v1-5 I declare my dependence on you. I reject the way of independence, of those who show no regard for you.

v6-9 **Praise the LORD** - he has heard. My heart trusts and I am helped. I leap for joy. A joyful heart never stops giving thanks, in any circumstance - I do not want to put out the fire of the Holy Spirit 1Thes 5:16-19.

PSALM 29 – The LORD is Enthroned as King

While this may be a song for the Temple there is also no greater place to sing it than in the midst of the creation.

v1,2 It is good for us mighty ones to understand the power of acknowledging the greatness of God – to praise your glory and worship in the splendour of your holiness.

v3-9 All things respond to your command. In your presence all creation cries 'Glory' - to the One who sits on the Throne and to the Lamb Rev 5:13. May we join with creation in this joy.

v10 You sit enthroned over the universe as king forever – with strength and peace. You wait for me to come into your presence!

PSALM 30 – You Have Turned My Mourning into Dancing!

David was prevented from building the Temple but set the tone of worship with this psalm 2Sam 7:1-6; 1Chr 22:7-9.

v1-3 I exalt you LORD, on the basis of past blessings.

v4-5 Weeping may remain for a night, but rejoicing comes in the morning – the end of our labour for the LORD is joy!

v6-10 I establish a positive confession when I am strong – so that it will be the basis for my confidence in the future.

v11 You change my situations - from sorrow into dancing and joy!

v12 You desire for me to sing to you and not be silent!

PSALM 31 - My Times are in Your Hands

v1-5 Into your hands I commit my spirit, every day and night v5.

v6-13 The lot of the servant of God – feet in a spacious place - though we may be required to suffer, to perfect our faith – we never give up 2Cor 4:16-18; Jas 1:2-4.

v14-18 You are my God - my times are in your hands. To know this axiom is of great strength to those who love the LORD.

v19-24 How great is your goodness and faithfulness, stored up for me. I am strong because my hope is in you.

PSALM 32 – My Sin Is Not Counted Against Me

v1,2 **Forgiveness** The blessing of having right standing with you – my sin covered, because of the shed blood of your Son, my Saviour and LORD Mt 26:28.

v3-5 I will not hide from you or keep silent. I acknowledged and confessed to you; you forgave the guilt of my sin 1Jn 1:9.

v6-7 You are my hiding place – you surround me with songs.

v8-11 You instruct, teach, counsel and watch over me – I will rejoice, sing and be glad, with a sincere heart.

PSALM 33 – I Wait in Hope, for You

v1-3 It is right to approach you LORD, with joy and praise - singing a new song of what you mean to me Eph 5:18-20.

v4,5 You are right, true, faithful and just, your love is unfailing.

v6-9 **By Your Word the Heavens were made** - by the breath of your mouth Heb 11:3. This fact counteracts the 'energy from nowhere, by chance' theory Pro 8:22-31.

v10,11 The plans of mankind are frustrated – your plans stand firm forever – they cannot be thwarted.

v12 There is need for national repentance and recommitment.

v13-19 You see and consider everything I do – you formed my heart v15! You keep me alive in all circumstances.

v20-22 As I wait in hope for you, your love rests upon me!

PSALM 34 – I Will Extol You - at all times

The way of the spirit-filled life Eph 5:18-20; Phil 4:6-7; 1Thes 5:16-29. David could experience this walk even when he was in utmost fear for his security and life 1Sam 21:10-15.

v1-3 Your praise will always be on my lips – a matter of the will.

v4-7 You deliver me from all my fears; you make me radiant; your angel camps around me!

v8-14 I have tasted and seen – you are good. You teach me awe and respect. I seek you and lack nothing v10.

v15-22 Your eyes are on me, you hear and deliver from all my troubles and all circumstances.

PSALM 35 – You Contend with my Enemy

v1-9 Defend me and my children from evil and the evil one, who is out to get me Is 49:25; Mt 6:13; Eph 6:12; 1Pet 5:8,9;.

v10-26 My whole being will exclaim, spirit, soul and body that you are my rescuer. I must be consistent in trust and faith as I wait for you to vindicate me in your righteousness v24; Jas 1:6-8.

v27,28 May all that I do and say be a source of praise to you.

PSALM 36 – Abundant Life Jn10:10

v1-4 I am led to pray for those who have no fear of you.

v5-7 You fill the universe with your presence and provision.

v8-12 I drink from your river of delights v8; Jn 4:13,14.

PSALM 37 – I Delight in You – I wait patiently

v1,2 You tell me not to fret or be envious of others - because you order my way and direct my path Pro 3:5-8; Mt 6:25-34.

v3-6 You say 'Trust in me, delight yourself in me, commit your way to me and I will give you the desires of your heart'.

v7-11 I will trust you, I will be still before you and wait for you v7,34; Is 40:31; 46:9-11. I will enjoy great peace v 11.

v12-40 I will delight in your way - though I stumble I will not fall for you uphold me with your hand v23,24.

PSALM 38 – I wait for You – You will Answer

v1 A petition – I can express my feelings and failures to you.

v2-14 I acknowledge my guilty feelings v4; you know my situation completely; nothing is hidden from you v9.

v15-18 The first steps out of guilt - I wait for you, I confess my wrongdoing and repent. You answer me 1Jn 1:8-10; 2:1,2.

v19-22 Do not leave me; keep me in your presence Ps 51:10-12.

PSALM 39 – The Discipline of Life

v1-8 The anguish of life, fleeting, but a breath, a phantom v6; Is 2:22. I wanted to know the outcome, but now I hope in you v7.

v9-11 When I withdraw from you I despair. Then I accept your rebuke and discipline – nothing happens outside of your will!

v12,13 I am an alien in this world, struggling with its ways. But I am with you - also a son and an heir! Gal 4:4-7.

PSALM 40 – I Desire to do Your Will, O LORD

v1 I waited patiently for you – you heard my cry.

v2,3 You lifted me, set me on a rock; put a song in my mouth.

v5-6 As I count my many blessings and your plans for me, both now and for eternity my trust grows stronger.

v6-10 Here I am, to do your will. This was fulfilled by your Son Jesus Christ Heb 10:5-10. May it be my goal in life.

v11-15 Trust requires persistence even in the face of adversity.

v16,17 I rejoice in you and say 'The LORD be exalted'.

PSALM 41 – I Have Regard for the Weak

v1-3 Blessed are the merciful for they will obtain mercy Mt 5:7. You deliver from trouble, work with me in all circumstances and restore me from illness v3 – you are my healer Ex 15:26.

v4-9 There are consequences to sin and wrong actions Rom 6:23.

v10-13 You set me in your presence – the promise of eternity!

PSALM 42 – Deep Calls to Deep - Spirit to spirit

Many struggle with a relationship with God because they are consumed by their circumstances, both good and bad. Jesus taught us that we will be filled with the Presence of God when we hunger and thirst for him Mt 5:6,8; Jer 29:11-13; 33:2.

v1-3 My soul longs, thirsts, pants for you O LORD – like a pursued deer. I want to be in your Presence.

v4-6 I remember the joy of times in your Presence. I tell my soul to remember and respond. There are times when we are physically and mentally discouraged – body and soul. Our spirit must take control based on God's promises and faithfulness.

v7 My spirit listens, Holy Spirit and hears you speak Gal 5:25.

v8-11 I seek your Presence in prayer and song – all through the day and night, God of my life, God my Rock!

PSALM 43 – I Will Go to Your Holy Mountain Heb 10:19

v1,2 When I feel things are against me – have you rejected me?

v3,4 Then I press in to your Presence, my joy and delight.

v5 The solution to my distress is to reaffirm my trust in you!

PSALM 44 – The Cost of Discipleship

v1-8 We remember past victories, both in your word and our own experiences when you delivered us and praise you forever.

v9-21 Sometimes we feel rejected and humbled as we have to suffer for the sake of the Gospel and because of evil Mt 5:11-16.

v22-26 Still we persevere and put our trust in you Rev 12:10-11.

PSALM 45 – Christ and His Church

This wedding song refers to the relationship between Jesus and the believer both now and in eternity Eph 5:25-32; Rev 19:7-9.

v1 **A wedding song** - a noble theme, of the great love of Jesus for his people – indeed a mystery! Eph 5:25-27, 32.

v2-8 **The Groom, Jesus** – you are most excellent, clothed with splendour and majesty - victorious.

v6,7 **Deity of Jesus** These words are spoken to the coming ruler *'Your throne, O God, will last forever v6.* Jesus has been set in the highest place by God v7 Phil 2:6-11; Heb 1:8.

v9-15 **The Bride, the believer** – at the right hand of the king v9. Honor to you for you are LORD v11.

v16,17 **The fruit of the harvest** – souls won for the kingdom.

PSALM 46 – Be Still and Know – I Am God

v1-3 You are my refuge, strength and ever present help - in every trouble. So I will not have fear in any situation.

v4,5 Holy Spirit you are my companion. The eternal City is my dwelling Rev 22:1-5. You make me glad!

v6,7 Nations are in uproar, kingdoms melt, there is conflict in every place. The best efforts of man are futile for they ignore you - their labour is but fuel for the fire Hab 2:13.

v8,9 I look forward to the day when the earth will be filled with the knowledge of your glory Is 2:4; Hab 2:14.

v10,11 I will be still - and know you – that you are God. I will exalt you - as you request – LORD Almighty Hab 2:20.

PSALM 47 – The Kings of Earth Belong to God

v1-4 I shout for joy – how awesome are you LORD Most High, great King over all the earth. You chose me and my inheritance! Rom 8:29-30; Eph 1:4,5.

v5,6 I sing praises to you for you will come again to rule.

v7-9 You are the King of heaven and earth - you reign over the nations. *The kingdom of the world will become the kingdom of our Lord and of his Christ and he will reign forever Rev 11:15.*

I am one of your nobles who will reign with you! V9; Rom 4:16; Gal 3:7-9; Rev 1:4-6.

PSALM 48 – Great is Your Presence, O LORD

Mt Zion is Jerusalem, city of God, city of the Great King, 87:1; 122:3-6; Is 46:13; 51:11 – it will be the joy of the whole earth.

v1-3 Your greatness is revealed in your Presence.

v4-8 All nations will see your glory and flee in terror Rev 1:7.

v9-14 I meditate in your presence, on your unfailing love.

PSALM 49 – The Cost of Redemption – Paid!

v1-6 Why should I fear - in any situation? Rom 5:8.

v7 We must stand before God – who can give a ransom to him?

v8,9 You paid the great ransom price for me so that I could have eternal life. Thank you! 2Cor 5:21; 8:9.

v10-14 There is no hope for man beyond the grave without you.

v15-20 You redeemed me by the death of your Son - you will take me to yourself!

PSALM 50 – I will Honor You, the Mighty One

v1-6 You summons all the earth to give account Rev 20:11-15.

v7-13 The world is yours and all that is in it. You do not need a sacrifice for everything is yours – every animal, bird and creature! What you ask of mankind is acknowledgment, thankfulness, relationship and commitment.

v14,15 I call on you, every day and I honor you.

v16-21 Words and outward show are of little use. Our actions reveal our heart and by them we will be called to account.

v23,23 I do give you thanks and I do honor you for you have shown me your salvation through Jesus.

PSALM 51 - Have mercy on me, O God - the path to forgiveness

This psalm was recorded when David was convicted over his great sin 2Sam 12:13. Despite the magnitude of his crime against people he saw his greatest sin as being against God v4.

It sets a pattern for our approach to God and our humble daily walk Mt 5:1-16. It also explains the basis for God's forgiveness and restoration.

v1 Petition – a plea for mercy – with no rights.

v2 Realisation that only God could forgive.

v3 Recognition – an awareness of sin, of the offense of sin to God.

v4-6 Confession – to admit - to come into agreement with God.

v7-9 Forgiveness – sorrow - a desire to be cleansed, forgiven, restored – only God can remove the stain and guilt.

v10-12 Repentance – a decision - a commitment to turn from sin.

v13,14 Restoration – the desire to be in relationship again - renewal comes from God.

v15-19 Thankfulness – a broken spirit and contrite heart v17.

David's great fear was that he would be cast from the Presence of God, that the Holy Spirit might leave him and that he might loose the joy of God's salvation v11,12.

This series of events may not have occurred if David had remained in active service for the LORD 2Sam 11:1.

PSALM 52 – I Flourish in Your House 1Sam 21:7, 22:9,8

David would have despaired when he learned that, in a senseless act, Saul had slaughtered the priests who had assisted him. There is no accounting for the evil in human nature. David held to his faith in God and pursued what is good.

v1-7 The end of the godless man – who chose to be in dependent, trusting in his own ability instead of putting his trust in you.

v8,9 The way of the saint – flourishing in your house, forever.

PSALM 53 – The Ultimate Trial of Life Rom 1:18-20

v1 **The fool says in his heart, 'There is no God'** The greatest folly is to look at the universe and all that is in it and to say it happened by chance. Science requires that every event has a cause. God is the ultimate, self-existing, eternal Cause of all things.

Science and evolution reveal the wonder of the Creator. Fools deny him in an effort to be independent.

The greatest test of life is to acknowledge God Rev 20:15.

v2-5 God looks for those who seek him 2Chr 16:9.

v6 Salvation has come out of Zion – with the life, death and resurrection of Jesus. I long for your reign – for salvation to be fulfilled at your second coming.

PSALM 54 – You are the One who Sustains Me

Even when betrayed by the people of Ziph, of the tribe of Judah, David's own clan, he trusted God Jos 15:55; 1Sam 23:19; 26:1.

v1-3 In the time of trouble, listen to my words – I must make you my first port of call before depending on others.

v4,5 We must recognise you are the source of our help Heb 11:6.

v6 I will praise you freely for you are good.

PSALM 55 – I Cast ALL My Cares on You 1Pet 5:7

v1-15 The anguished heart, when my thoughts trouble me.

v16-21 When I call on you, evening, morning and noon you ransom me unharmed. You hear from your eternal throne v19.

v22,23 I trust you completely because you will never let me fall. When I cast all my cares on you I am freed from anxiety.

PSALM 56 – You Let Me Walk in the Light of Life

In the hands of his enemy, the Philistines, David maintained his faith 1Sam 21:10; Ps 34:1-22; Jn 8:12.

v1-11 When I am afraid (seized by foe) - I will trust in you and your Word v4. You have promised to be with me and provide for me and I believe it Rom 10:17; Heb 11:6. What can man do to me?

v12,13 I have promised to thank you because you always deliver me and light my path in all areas of life.

PSALM 57 - You have a Purpose for Me!
David had the opportunity to kill Saul but continued to trust God's ways 1Sam 22:1; 24:3-7; Ps 105:15.

v1 I am not in a cave – but in the shadow of your wings 63:7. My situation does not depend on location by on your Presence.

v2 You will fulfil your purpose for me Jer 29:11-14; Eph 2:10.

v3,4 Despite the problems and the circumstances, I will praise you.

v5 *Be exalted, O God above the heavens; let your glory be over all the earth.* A good song for a cave, in trouble!

v6,7 I have a steadfast heart so I will song and make music.

v8-10 I wake my soul and I wake the dawn, with singing and praise to you O LORD among the nations.

v11 Be exalted, O God, above the heavens and earth – be exalted in my heart.

PSALM 58 – You are the Judge of the Earth Rev 20:11-13
v1-11 God has revealed his moral order within the heart of each person. Therefore mankind is without excuse Rom 1:18-21.

v10,11 We can be confident that God's justice will be applied. I know the righteous are still rewarded for you are Judge of the earth.

PSALM 59 – O My Strength, I Sing Praise to You
Saul issued a death warrant on David but it had no effect on the LORD'S anointed 1Sam 19:1.

v1-8 When I am surrounded by trouble you laugh at those who would harm me – they cannot go beyond your will.

v9-17 I watch for you – my Strength, my fortress, my loving God.

PSALM 60 – We will Gain the Victory 1Chro 19:6-19
Several nations united against David but were trampled down v12.

v1-5 Even in desperate times you have raised a banner over me.

v6-12 You have spoken – you will keep the promises of your Word – with you I gain the victory.

PSALM 61 – I Long to Dwell in Your Tent
David made a tent for the Ark and communed with God 2Sam 6:17.

v1-4 You are the rock that is higher than me. Moses found this place, a rock near God - we can go and stand there whenever we want Ex 33:18-23. I want to dwell in your Presence.

v5 My heritage is the right to stand in your Presence.

v6-8 **Enthroned in your presence** – This promise applies to Jesus where is now seated. But it also applies for the believer, made possible by his death and resurrection Rev 1:6.

PSALM 62 – My Soul Finds Rest - in You Alone
v1-10 I rest in you for there is no confidence in any other. My salvation an my honor depend on you v7.

v11,12 God has revealed that he is strong and loving. Judgement is sure – salvation is through Christ alone Rom 3:21-24.

PSALM 63 – In the Shadow of Your Wings 1Sam 23:29
This is one of the most beautiful expressions of the personal walk with God - a guide to all who would seek him. It was composed in the desert!
v1 A declaration! You are my God, earnestly I seek you – I thirst for you and long for you more than anything else.

v2 I have seen you in your power and your glory – in creation, in your Presence and in my heart.

v3-5 Your love is better than life so I will glorify you with singing lips. I will praise you as long as I live and my soul will be satisfied with your rich provision.

v6 I remember you and think of you, meditating when I go to bed and get up and when I wake up through the night 139:17,18.

v7 Because you are the one who helps me I sing as I am always in the shadow of your wings.

v8-11 My soul clings to you and you uphold me.

PSALM 64 – All will Proclaim Your Works
v1-10 When I suffer injustice I turn to you.

v9 I remember that all will stand before you and bow the knee.

v10 I take refuge in you and I rejoice.

PSALM 65 – You Chose Me!
v1 I wait for you, in praise and worship – as I look for your Presence and deliverance.

v2,3 While I was still a sinner you forgave my transgressions by sending Jesus to die in my place and rise again Rom 5:8.

v4 You chose me and brought me into a relationship with you and you fill me with good things.

v5-8 I praise you with joy - especially as I rise and retire.

v9-13 You provide me with abundance from the earth you created.

PSALM 66 – Shout For Joy

v1-9 I shout and sing for joy – how awesome are your deeds.

v10-17 You test me and refine me 1Pet 6-9. You delivered me and brought me to a place of abundance.

v18-20 Grant me a clean heart that does not cherish sin.

PSALM 67 – May Your Face Shine on Me

v1,2 Grace - God's free unmerited favour, based on the Giver, not the response - all we have, are and hope for!

Bless me that I may make your ways known 1Chr 4:9:10

v3,4 May my thankful, joyful life, filled with praise, be used to lead others to you Mt 5:16.

v6,7 May we know your blessing and the ends of the earth fear you.

PSALM 68 – You are Awesome, O God

v1-3 You are awesome in your works and in your power to protect.

v4-17 I praise and extol you. I rejoice before you. You fill the universe, defend the disadvantaged and provide for your people.

v18 When you ascended you gave gifts and power to the Church Eph 4:7-13. This passage was used in reference to Jesus.

v19-23 You daily bear my burdens and keep me from harm.

v24-27 Your Kingship has been revealed Mt 21:5.

v28-35 We call on your power today to establish your kingdom on earth and to bring about the return of Jesus.

PSALM 69 – We will Gain the Victory

Here also is reference to Jesus v9,21; Mt 21:12-17; Jn 2:17.

v1-5 When I am worn out calling for help with nothing to commend myself – in the midst of great suffering – for the guilt of others!

v6-12 The zeal of God was required to work my salvation.

v12-21 Prayer is not only for deliverance but for strength to perseverance. Nothing could relieve the depth of suffering v21.

v22-28 Jesus died so that the judgment of God may be removed for

v30-36 I will praise and glorify your name with thanksgiving for your salvation which protects me, and my children.

PSALM 70 – I Rejoice and I Am Glad
v1-3 We may be persecuted and criticised to the point of despair.
v4,5 Even as I wait to be saved I say be exalted, O God in my life.

PSALM 71 – I Always Have Hope
v1-7 You are my confidence, from the beginning, to the end v17,18.
v8-14 My mouth is filled with your praise. I will never give up and will praise you more and more 2Cor 4:16-18.
v15-18 I will tell of your salvation – to the next generation.
v19-24 My lips shout for joy and will tell I have been redeemed!

PSALM 72 – Jesus is the Eternal King
v1-16 These statements are fulfilled in Jesus – justice, a royal son, ruler and righteous judge Is 11:1-5; 60:1-22; 61:1-11. All kings will bow down to him and all nations will serve him Rev 19:11-17.
v17 The promise of God to Abraham that all peoples on earth will be blessed through him has been fulfilled Gen 12:2,3; Rom 4:16,17.
v18-20 I praise you, LORD God, forever, for the whole earth will be filled with your glory Hab 2:13,14..

PSALM 73 – I Enter Your Sanctuary – then I understand
v1 I know that you are good Ex 33:19; Eph 2:7; Jas 1:17.
v2-12 Sometimes I become envious that the wicked seem to prosper v3. They ignore you saying that you do not know v11.
v13-15 I feel that despite my best efforts I am being punished and that nothing is going right. I keep my thoughts to myself.
v16,17 When I come into your Presence, then I understand – the just will live by his faith in you Hab 2:4. You must test my trust in you and my faith to prove that it is genuine Heb 11:6; 1Pet 1:7-9.
v18-22 I had the false perception that those who do wrong might go unpunished – suddenly you will return and call them to account.
v23-28 As for me, I know it is good to be near you and my faith is renewed – for you, the Sovereign LORD is my refuge.

PSALM 74 – You, O God, Are My King
v1-11 When I feel rejected – the evil one would crush me v8.
v12-21 I recall who you are, what you have done. You brought salvation. You provided the sea, the day and night, the seasons. You set all the boundaries that created and maintain the universe! v17.

v22,23 Rise up, O God and defend your cause, we trust in you.

PSALM 75 – You Bring Down and Exalt
v1-3 I give thanks to you, O God for it is you who chooses the appointed time – to live and die, to act and give account.
You judge uprightly and hold the pillars of the earth firm.
v4-10 You are sovereign, you bring one down, exalt another, the righteous will be exalted. The cup of wrath will come Rev 16:1.

PSALM 76 – Resplendent, Majestic - My God
v1-4 You are the source of light, more majestic than creation.
v5-12 From heaven you govern the earth. You are sovereign over all mankind – rulers and afflicted alike.

PSALM 77 – I Will Remember and Meditate On You
v1-9 In difficult times, to remember the good times is hard.
v10-12 Then I remember you! I meditate on you and on your mighty deeds of the past – yes, on what you have done for me!
v13-20 I remember who you are – holy, the God of miracles and power v13. I remember how you redeemed me v14.

PSALM 78 - Your Praiseworthy Deeds – I remember them
v1-8 Talk about what God has done. Tell our children about his wonders so that they will put their trust in him v4,7.
v9-16 Despite God's guidance and provision the people did not keep their relationship with him and refused to live by his ways.
v17-31 They rebelled against God and put him to the test. They spoke against him despite the evidence of his ongoing provision.
v32-55 The cycle of God's faithfulness, the sin of the people and God's renewed mercy is often repeated. He blesses the good and bad yet many continue to deny and reject him and his ways.
v56-59 They chose to deny him in order to live their own lives.
v60-64 They lost the Ark in battle and the LORD abandoned Shiloh – his Presence left their place of worship.
v65-72 A faithful king has come from Judah – Jesus!

PSALM 79 – I Am a Sheep In Your Pasture
v1-4 I am in desperate need. People of the world have denied you and are changing your laws for ways that suit themselves.

v5-8 We are in desperate need for you to turn us back to your ways. In your mercy come quickly to meet us.

v9-12 Help us, for the glory of your name! Forgive our sins.

v13 For I am your sheep – you are my Shepherd.

PSALM 80 – You Make Your Face Shine on Me

v1-3 I appeal to the highest authority – enthroned in heaven.

v4-16 It seems like everything is against me, again.

v17,18 Now we know the Son of Man! The One at your right hand – who you have raised up for us. You have revived us!

PSALM 81 – I Open My Mouth for You to Fill

v1-5 I sing for joy and shout aloud to you my strength.

v6-12 You blessed your people but they would not listen to you; they ignored you, denied you and chose to live independently.

v13-16 I listen to you and follow your ways. You satisfy me with the finest of blessings and honey from the rock.

PSALM 82 – I Am a Son of the Most High!

v1 God of gods! There is no other god. You are sovereign above all authority and rulers of the earth and all philosophies of man.

v2-5 People live for themselves and make laws that are selfish and unjust, corrupt and immoral and contrary to your ways.

v6-8 I am your child, your inheritance - you sent Jesus to redeem me so I could be adopted Jn 1:12; Jn 1:12,13; Eph 1:4-6; Gal 4:7.

PSALM 83 – You Alone are the Most High

v1-4 People of the world are antagonistic. They cast off constraint by denying you and your Word Mt 24:24; 2Pet 3:3.

v5-8 As the surrounding nations came against Israel so your people are persecuted by the world today.

v9-17 You delivered your people in the past.

v18 You will reveal yourself in justice and righteousness.

PSALM 84 – How Lovely is Your Dwelling Place

Here is another pattern for personal devotion and fellowship.

v1 How I have learned to enjoy your Presence – in prayer, song, meditation and reading your Word, O LORD Almighty.

v2 I yearn, faint and cry out – to be with you, the living God.

v3-4 I will be ever praising you (with the sparrow).

v5-9 For those who set their hearts on you, the path of prayer and worship leads to springs in the desert. Tears turn to blessings, going from strength to strength, appearing before you v7.

v10,11 Better to be with you than anywhere else. You withhold no good thing from those who seek you, my sun and shield.

v12 LORD, teach me to want to pray, to draw near to your Most Holy Place, often, to learn to commune with you Heb 10:19-22.

PSALM 85 – Revive Us Again, O LORD

v1-5 A call to prayer for our city, nation and generation, our leaders in government and church 126:4-6; 1Tim 2:1-4.

v6-7 As we see people reject God's Word, deny his Person and his Son Jesus. As we see the conflict within the nations.

A cry for revival in our time – that God may visit us with salvation - out of his unfailing love - that we might rejoice with him over souls saved. O that we might dwell in unity 133:1-3 – coming together across denominations to pray for the city.

v8-9 Surely your salvation is near, you do not want any to perish - so I will petition you 67:1,2; Is 56:6,7; 2 Pet 3:9.

v10-11 God's righteousness and peace, justice and mercy, holiness and love kiss at the cross of Jesus Eph 2:13,14.

v12-13 The LORD will indeed give us a good harvest - of souls.

PSALM 86 – Give Me an Undivided Heart

v1-4 I lift up my soul even when joy is gone and focus on you.

v5-10 You alone are God – there is none like you. There will be peace on earth when Jesus comes to reign v9; Is 2:2-4; Rev 20:4.

v11-17 Teach me to walk with an undivided heart v11.

PSALM 87 – I Am a Citizen of Zion – the city of God

v1,2 You have chosen Zion as your dwelling, your City O God. This is the reason Israel continues to claim Jerusalem (from 1000 BC) 48:1; 122:6,7. There will be a new Jerusalem Rev 21:1-5.

v3,4 Of the great cities of Egypt, Babylon, Philistia, Tyre and Ethiopia the greatest privilege is to be identified with your city.

v5-7 You gave me the desire to belong to you and the means – by faith in Jesus 1Pet 2:4-10; Heb 12:22.

PSALM 88 – My Heart is Open Before You
v1-9 Day and night I cry out before you - every day v1,9.
v10-18 I begin the day telling you what I think. I praise you and put my plans before you. I seek your direction and follow it.

PSALM 89 – I Have Learned to Acclaim You! 2Sam 7:4-16
v1-4 You, O LORD are faithful forever. I declare it! Your Covenant with Abraham and David means that Jesus will reign forever 1Chr 17:10-14. I will be part of that kingdom.
v5-14 All things are yours. You are faithful, righteous and just.
v15-18 Here is the discipline for a victorious and effective life -
• to learn to acclaim you, applaud you, recognise your blessing in my life and give you praise and thanks. Praise the LORD!
• to walk in your presence, moment by moment
• to rejoice in your name all day long, always giving you praise and thanks as you work out your purpose in my life
• to exult and be excited in your righteousness, in right standing with you – by faith in Christ alone Rom 1:16,17, 3:21-24
• to make you my glory and strength - to put you first and depend on you above and before all else
• then to find that you exalt me – you lift me up – you fill me with joy and expectation as I believe in you Rom 15:13.
v19-29 The LORD's commitment to David in this prophetic promise has been fulfilled in Jesus Christ Is 9:6,7; Lk 1:30-33.
v30-37 The Throne of David will be established forever.
v38-49 The physical line of kings failed until Jesus Rev 5:9,10.
v50-52 The suffering of Christ was required to bring salvation and eternal life for me! 1Cor 2:7; Eph 1:4; 2Tim 1:9.
Praise be to the LORD forever!

PSALM 90 – Establish the Work of My Hands
v1,2 From everlasting to everlasting, you are the eternal God.
v3-10 Finite, natural man returns to dust - trouble, sorrow and we quickly fly away. There is no hope of life beyond the grave.
v4 Eternal life is received only through Jesus v4; 1Jn 5:11,12.
v11-15 Teach me to plan my days to gain a wise heart.
v16,17 Let your blessing rest on my family and my deeds.

PSALM 91 – You Are My Dwelling, Most High

v1 O the joy of learning to dwell in your presence - in your shadow, Most High – wherever I am Mt 28:20.

v2-8 You provide your provision and protection in all things.

9-14 I can actually dwell with you in my daily life, in every situation. May I never depart!

v10-15 You command protection in everything I do for you.

v16 You have shown me your salvation Acts 2:38,39; 16:31.

PSALM 92 - It is Good to Make Music to You

v1-3 I express my joy to you in the morning and in the night to remind me of what you will do and of what you have done.

v4,5 You make me glad by your presence in my life.

v6-15 I want to flourish in your courts, O God, staying fresh and green, proclaiming your name, and always bear fruit v12,13.

PSALM 93 – The Lord Reigns in Majesty!

v1 I see you in creation, your majesty and power.

v2 You are eternal, your throne was established before time.

v5 I acknowledge your Person and nature, O LORD and you Word - the only eternal realities in my existence.

PSALM 94 – I am Blessed by Your Discipline

v1-11 There is a difference between discipline and punishment.

v12-23 Blessed is the man you discipline and teach your Law.

v19 Joy replaces anxiety when we turn to you Mt 6:25-34.

PSALM 95 – Come Let Us Sing and Bow Down

v1-5 **Celebration - I want to sing for joy -** to shout aloud, to give thanks to you and extol you with music and song, great God and great King. You are sovereign over the universe and in control of all things including my every situation.

v6,7 **Worship - I want to bow down in worship -** and kneel before you O LORD, my Maker – in awe and wonder at your splendour, greatness and your holiness – at your mercy displayed in the cross. You are my God and I am a sheep, under your care.

v8-11 **Only then can I really know you and know your rest** Heb 4:11 – when I learn to worship you for who you are and celebrate your goodness to me, in all areas of my life.

PSALM 96 – The Splendour of Your Holiness

v1-6 I sing to you a new song because of your greatness. I see your majesty in the creation, but particularly in your Presence.

v7-9 I ascribe greatness to you I consciously recognise it. I worship and tremble in the splendour of your holiness.

v10-13 **The LORD reigns** – in creation and the affairs of man.

I look forward to you coming to reign, Lord Jesus Rev 11:15.

PSALM 97 – You Are Exalted Far Above All

v1-9 You reign over all – in righteousness and justice, power and glory – I am glad and I rejoice, O LORD, Most High!

v10-12 Be exalted and reign - in my heart and in my life.

PSALM 98 - You are Coming to Judge the Earth

v1-3 You have revealed your plan of salvation for all nations.

v4-9 I am excited and shout for joy for you are coming to rule and judge the earth in righteousness and with equity.

PSALM 99 - I Worship – at Your Footstool

v1-4 You are exalted, awesome, holy and worthy of praise.

v5 I exalt you, LORD my God and worship at your footstool.

v6-9 Moses and Aaron were priests. Now I am a priest and you call me to worship in your holy presence Is 61:2; 1Pet 2:9.

PSALM 100 – I Come with Thanksgiving

v1,2 The joy of your presence – I must express it, with gladness.

v3 I know you are good. You made me, I belong to you. I am the sheep of your pasture. You are my Shepherd!

v4-5 I enter your Presence in the morning with thankfulness and praise because of your goodness, love and your faithfulness.

PSALM 101 – I Walk with a Blameless Heart

v1-3 Part of my worship is to set before my eyes no vile thing.

v4-8 Every morning I will commit to walk in your ways.

PSALM 102 – You Remain the Same

These words encourage the believer. They also apply to Jesus.

v1-11 I am in distress – life seems so short, so futile, so variable.

v12-17 You respond to my prayer and bring salvation.

v18-22 You are eternal and your promises continue in all generations. From your Throne you see, hear and release. You released prisoners from sin and everlasting separation, when you sent your Son to remove the offense of sin Lk 4:18-21.

v23,24 This plea could relate to the cry from the cross Mt 27:46.

v25-28 **The promise of eternal life** The reply from God the Father confirms the deity of the Son Heb 1:10-12. The eternal life of the believer is also assured v28.

PSALM 103 – Praise The Lord, O My Soul

v1 Praise is a matter of the will – I must bring my soul to praise you and my body! This is the demand of the born again spirit. The Bible reveals the human being as a unity - whole spirit, soul and body 1 Thes 5:23. When a person accepts Jesus Christ as Savior and Lord the spirit within is regenerated – born again, by the operation of the Holy Spirit who then dwells within Jn 1:12,13; 3:3-8; Eph 1:13,14.

v2 I WILL remember all your benefits to me – a cause for praise.

v3-5 You forgive my sins, heal my diseases, redeem me from disasters, crown me with love, satisfy my desires with good things and renew my youth like an eagle! Praise the LORD!

v6-12 You do not treat me as my sins deserve. Your forgiveness is absolute.

v13-16 You take into account my frailty because I am but dust.

v17-18 Your commitment to those who fear you is eternal. May your blessing be on my children and children's children.

v19-22 So I will praise you, obey your Word and seek to do your will, like the angels in heavens and all your creation.

PSALM 104 – You Are Very Great

v1-4 You are clothed with splendour and majesty. Creation reveals your glory – vast because of the vastness of your glory.

v5-29 You made and sustain all things that exist.

v29-30 At the birth of each individual you send your Spirit to bring them life. You breathe into man to give him your image. You take away breath, the soul, and he returns to dust – the cosmic elements out of which he was formed Job 12:10.

v31-35 I will sing to you all my life. May my meditation be pleasing to you as I rejoice in you!

PSALM 105 – I Always Seek Your Face

v1-4 The source of my joy is that I always seek your face.

v5-7 We are encouraged to remember what God has done in the past, in history and in our own lives 1Cor 10:11.

v8-14 It is good to review God's faithfulness to Abraham and his people and the Exodus – also recounted in Psalms 106, 135 and 136. We can learn from their blessings and mistakes.

v15 **Do not touch my Anointed** We must respect the anointing of God on the lives of others. It is God who appoints and deposes Dan 2:20,21. It is not by strength that one prevails – the LORD gives strength and exalts his anointed 1Sam 2:9,10; 24:6.

v16-22 Joseph prospered in Egypt under God's provision and anointing – from prisoner to Prime Minister Gen 37 to 41.

v23-36 The Israelites were delivered by the ten plagues against the pantheon of Egyptian gods Ex 7:4. The plagues were in the form of natural disasters with the timing and severity by the hand of God. They were intended to gain the commitment of the people to their supreme YHWH Ex 15:11; 18:11; 20:2,3.

v37-45 God brought Israel through their training, out of bondage in Egypt and demonstrated his faithfulness that they might keep his precepts and observe his laws – Praise the LORD.

PSALM 106 – Your Love Endures Forever

v1-2 I give thanks for who you are and what you have done.

v3 Our response to the favour of God is to live by his ways.

v4-47 **You are Faithful** A reminder of God's faithfulness despite our failings based on a further review of the Exodus.

When we see that the purpose of our trials is to develop our faith and trust in God we can look ahead with a positive attitude like Joshua and Caleb despite the unpleasant times Nu 14:7-9.

It will go on until we are not lacking anything Jas 1:2-4.

v33 We must realise the consequences of rebelling against the Spirit of God Rom 12:11; Eph 4:30; 1Thes 5:19.

v48 We can look forward to eternity when we accept God's son Jesus Christ, as Savior and Lord Jn 3:16.

PSALM 107 – The Redeemed of the Lord - Let Us Say So!

A review of the good things God has done for his people in the past – through events in all areas of life.

v1-2 Let those who are redeemed say so! I must declare it to all.

v3-9 Those lost in life, when they cried out to the LORD in their trouble, he rescued and led to a safe place to live.

v10-16 Captives in prison for their wrongdoing, when they called out, he broke down the doors and restored them.

v17-22 Those who suffered affliction because of their rebellion were healed – there is healing in the Word of God v20.

v23-32 Seafarers were delivered from mighty storms at sea.

v33-38 Those who suffered famine because of their wrongdoing, when they repented he returned to times of plenty.

v39-42 Those who encounter all kinds of oppression, calamity and sorrow will be delivered when they seek the LORD and his ways – they will see and rejoice.

v43 It is good wisdom, to take notice of these things – the goodness of God and his promises and apply them.

PSALM 108 – Your Faithfulness Is Great

v1-5 My heart is steadfast in praising you, O God. For your great love is higher than the heavens and your faithfulness reaches to the skies. Be exalted in my life and in my heart.

v6-13 With you I will gain the victory.

PSALM 109 – I Am a Man of Prayer

v1-5 I praise you and do not remain silent. I am persistent in coming before you for I am a man of prayer Is 62:6,7.

v6-29 We are encouraged to pray for all men, even those who mistreat us. In so doing we may see their salvation Mt 5:43-48.

v30,31 With my mouth I will greatly extol you - continually.

PSALM 110 – The LORD Says To My LORD!

v1 David prophesied this psalm about Jesus. The LORD God anointed David's LORD Jesus to sit at God's right hand Heb 1:13. Jesus used this psalm to confirm that he is the Son of God Mt 22:41-46. It was also quoted by Peter Acts 2:29-36.

v2,3 The eternal rule of Jesus is coming Rev 19:11-16.

v4-7 Another prophetic statement regarding Jesus – he will be prophet, priest and king forever Heb 7:17. He will be judge v6.

PSALM 111 – I Extol You for who you are
v1 Teach me how to extol you - with all my heart.

v2-8 I praise you for who you are and what you have done.

v9 Thank you for sending Jesus to redeem me! v9.

v10 I fear you, in reverent awe and will seek wisdom and understanding by reading your Word Prov 1:7; 2:5,6; 9:10.

PSALM 112 – I Find Great Delight in You
v1 Because I recognise who you are I will great delight in reading your Word and following you commands 1:1-3.

v2-5 I look to you for your continued blessing on my family and my life Mt 6:33. I will be generous with my time and resources.

v6-8 I will never be shaken – I will have no fear of the world because my heart is steadfast and secure in you.

v9,10 I will be generous and do what is right in your sight.

PSALM 113 – Sun Up to Dusk - Praise You
v1-3 Praise will be given to you – for eternity 50:1.

v4-6 Sovereign LORD, exalted over all nations, your glory is above the heavens – you are enthroned on high – may I see you and praise you always. You stoop down to relate to me.

v7-9 You meet the needs of the poor, the needy and oppressed.

PSALM 114 – I Tremble at Your Presence
v1-6 Israel was brought out of bondage in Egypt with a mighty hand that they might revere God and follow his ways Ex 6:6-8.

v7.8 Reverential fear and respect of the Creator is the beginning of wisdom and good sense when I consider who you are Pr 9:10.

One day all will acknowledge you and bow down Phil 2:9-11.

PSALM 115 – The Highest Heavens are Yours
v1 I worship you, in spirit and in truth Jn 4:23,24.

v3-15 Others may deny you, but I acknowledge and trust in you.

v16-18 All creation belongs to you – but you have given earth to man – we will be accountable. I extol you, now and forevermore.

PSALM 116 – I Believe – So I Act!
v1-2 I love you LORD and will call on you as long as I live.

v3-6 In trouble I called on your name and you saved me.

v7 My soul is at rest once more for you have been good to me.

v8-11 Even when I felt afflicted I held to my confidence in you.

v10 **This is the way that all faith works -**

• when I act on what I believe from the promises in your Word you are faithful to fulfil it in my situation Rom 10:17. I believe therefore I have spoken Acts 4:19,20

• I believe you sent Jesus to die for my sins and to rise again so that I might have eternal life - I believed and am saved Jn 3:16

• in the same way I testify about Jesus and the good news of the Gospel – I believe it and so I tell others.

v12-19 How can I thank you for your goodness - you have freed me from my chains – I will praise you and serve you.

PSALM 117 – Your Eternal Faithfulness

v1,2 I extol you and will declare your love and faithfulness continually. This simple declaration is the testimony of all believers. It applies for all nations Mt 28:18-20; Acts 1:8.

PSALM 118 – You Are My God – I Exalt You

This is a triumphal procession of a king and his people, approaching the Temple to give thanks to God for the victory and requesting continued provision. It was possibly for David's coronation but prophetically describes the entry of Jesus into Jerusalem on Palm Sunday, as perceived by the common people when they would make him king Mt 21:1-11; Lk 19:40.

v1-4 Thank you, for your love endures forever. I declare it to all.

v5-7 You give me great confidence to act as I serve you.

v8-14 It is better to trust you than anyone or anything else.

v15-21 You have become my salvation – I have entered your Presence and will give thanks with shouts of joy and victory.

v22,23 **The Living Stone** The stone rejected by the builders has become the centre block of the arch. David was rejected by Saul and eventually became king. Jesus was rejected by the religious leaders and is now King of kings. When they asked Jesus to tell the people to stop acknowledging him he quoted this text Mt 21:42. Jesus is the living stone and we have become living stones that cry out his praise – to us he is precious Lk 19:28; 1Pet 4-10.

v24 The LORD made the day that Jesus brought salvation. He makes every day new – let us rejoice and be glad in it.

v25 *O LORD, save us* – this equates to 'Hosanna', the cry of the people to Jesus as he entered Jerusalem Mt 21:9

v26 *Blessed is he who comes in the name of the LORD* – the recognition of Jesus as king by the people Mt 21:9

v27 The LORD has provided the light of his salvation – join in the procession of thanksgiving Lk 2:29-32.

v28,29 You are my God – I thank you and will exalt you.

PSALM 119 – Your Eternal Word – My Treasure!

There are 176 verses – every one of them stressing **the importance of God's Word to my daily life** Jos 1:8; Jn 15:3,8. **The Word of God** – His Laws, Testimonies, Precepts, Statutes, Commands, Ordinances and Decrees. Do not forget his Promises – not just commands but assurances, encouragement, guidance and direction. Here are just some examples of application, all confirmed in the New Testament -

v1,2 There is blessing when I walk according to your Word.

v9 How do I keep my way pure - by living by your Word.

v10 I seek you with all my heart – do not let me stray from your Word.

v11 I have hid your Word in my heart - that I might not sin against you.

v14 I rejoice in following your Word – as in great riches.

v16 I delight in your Word – I will not neglect your Word.

v18 Open my eyes to see – wonderful things in your Word.

v32 I run in the path of your Word – you have set my heart free.

v35 Direct me in your Word – there I find delight.

v47 I delight in your Word – I love it.

v50 My comfort in suffering – your Word preserves me.

v62 At midnight I rise to give you thanks – for your Word.

v66 Teach me – for I believe your Word.

v68 You are good, what you do is good – teach me your Word.

v89 Your Word is eternal - it stands firm in the heavens.

v91 Your Word endures - for all things serve you.

v97 How I love your Word – I meditate on it all day long.

v103 How sweet is your Word to my taste - sweeter than honey!

v105 Your Word is a lamp to my feet – a light for my path.

v114 You are my refuge shield - I put my hope in your Word.

v120 My flesh trembles in reverent fear of you – I stand in awe and respect of your Word.

v136 Tears flow from my eyes – for your Word is not obeyed.

v161 My heart trembles – at your Word.

v162 I rejoice in your promises - I find great spoil in your Word.

v171 My lips overflow with praise – you teach me your Word.

v176 When I strayed – I did not forget your Word.

PSALM 120 – I am a Man of Peace

This is the first of fourteen ascent psalms possibly used when ascending into Jerusalem and the Temple courts for worship 24:3; 122:1. Most psalms can be used in this way as we approach the LORD, from our circumstances to his Presence.

v1 This is the normal response to distress. Anxiety is not a practical option – it achieves nothing Mt 6:25,32-34.

v2-6 We desire to be free from those who ignore God's Word.

v7 Blessed are the peacemakers – they are called the children of God Mt 5:9. We bring peace with God to man and his fellows.

PSALM 121 – My Help Comes From My Maker

v1,2 Why should I look to others to save me? You have made all things. Help me to look to you first - in all things Mt 6:33.

v3,4 You do not slumber or sleep and you watch over me!

v5.6 You protect me through the day and the night.

v7 You keep me from all harm. You watch over my coming and going both now and forevermore!

PSALM 122 – Let Us Go into Your House!

v1 I am so glad to be in your presence with others Heb 12:22-24. One of the reasons people have a problem with church is that they go to be entertained rather than to meet with the living God.

v2 I want to be a person of prayer and praise Is 2:3.

v3-5 Jerusalem is the capital of Israel and has been from antiquity 87:1; Gen 12:1-3; 2Sam 5:6,7.

v6-8 I pray for Jerusalem and your people Israel, for the Church and for the people of the world v8; 1Tim 2:1-4.

PSALM 123 – I Lift Up My Eyes To Your Throne

v1-2 What a privilege to pray to you whose throne is in heaven, our Master, the LORD our God – and to wait on you Is 40:31.

v3,4 I look to you because your mercy is sure.

PSALM 124 - If You Had Not Been On My Side
v1 I praise you, LORD – for I am on your side!

v2-5 It is good to acknowledge you are my source of success.

v6-7 It is good to give thanks to God, and praise, especially when we are saved from disaster or a particular problem.

v8 My friend and my LORD is the Maker of heaven and earth!

PSALM 125 – I Trust In You – Like a Mountain
v1-2 Jerusalem was a well fortified city. I cannot be shaken because you surround me, always, as I trust in you.

v3-5 Bad associations lead to distraction from what is right. We must ask for God's provision to be upright.

PSALM 126 – Sow In Tears, Reap In Joy
When the exiles returned from captivity in Babylon they were filled with laughter and joy at what God had done for them. We must commit to God in the good times as well as the bad 137:1.

v1-3 You do great things for me – even though I have to go through tough times. You have filled my mouth with laughter and my tongue with songs of joy Is 61:1-3,10.

v4 Revive us again O Lord that we may rejoice in you 85:6,7.

v5 I will sow in tears for I know I will reap in joy.

v6 I share the Gospel with others in order to bring in the sheaves.

PSALM 127 – I Build in Vain Without You
v1 I want to build with you, in everything I do – to stand and watch with you. I remember that it is your work I am involved with and that I must be responsive to your Holy Spirit Zec 4:6.

v2 Grant me sweet sleep as I meditate on you.

v3-5 My children are your reward – I will not be put to shame.

PSALM 128 – You Bless My House, O Lord
v1 I do fear you, awesome LORD and walk in all your ways.

v2-4 I am forever thankful for all your blessings to me!

v5,6 May my family know your blessing as well.

PSALM 129 – I Bless Others In Your Name
v1-7 Many cause oppression but you set me free from such people and their actions. I do not get involved with those who promote evil nor do I seek their recognition.

v8 But I can bless others in your name because I am a child of the blessing – and I do! Gal 3:14.

PSALM 130 – With You there is Forgiveness

v1,2 I am in deep trouble again – out of the depths I cry to you. v3,4 **Forgiveness** If you kept a record of sins who could stand. But with you there is forgiveness 1Jn 1:8 to 2:2; Rev 20:11-15.

v5-6 I wait for you and put my hope in your Word.

v7,8 With you there is unfailing love and full redemption.

PSALM 131 – I Submit Humbly to You

v1,2 My heart is not proud - I humbly and quietly commit myself to you and your will for my life Pro 3;5-8.

v3 I have learned contentment as I trust in you Phil 4:12,13.

PSALM 132 – I Have Made a Place for You – in My Heart

v1-5 Like David I seek to put you first, in all things Mt 6:33.

v6-13 Zion is your dwelling – I want to be there Heb 12:22. Jesus is your anointed One, I want to know him more.

v14-16 You have chosen Zion and desired it for your dwelling. You include me in your resting place, forever Rev 21:1-5. You have blessed me abundantly and clothed me with salvation – I will ever sing for joy Is 51:11; Jn 7:37,38; Rev 21:3,4.

v17-18 The crown of Jesus is resplendent Rev 5:5.

PSALM 133 – The LORD Bestows His Blessing

v1 O that your people, all believers, could work together in unity Eph 4:1-6. How good and pleasing it would be, for you and for them! One message, one purpose, one effort - no division or conflict Jn 17:21; Eph 4:1-6. There would be one choice for the people of the world – Jesus or everlasting separation.

v2-3 The blessing would be much greater than the anointing of Aaron or the dew of mighty Mt Hermon falling on Mt Zion – there would be blessing in abundance – revival in out time.

v3 For there you commanded your blessing – even eternal life.

PSALM 134 – I Will Praise You, Unceasingly

v1-3 What a joy to praise you, both day and night. I have time at night when other activities are done. I lift up my hands in your presence and praise you. I know your Presence v3.

PSALM 135 – I Minister In Your Presence!

v1 You have chosen me to minister before you and to serve you – a member of a royal priesthood to praise you 1Pet 2:5.

v3-4 I am your treasured possession, out of all the earth 1Pet 2:9.

v5-18 You are greater than all the world has to offer – to me.

v19-21 That is why I praise and worship you, O LORD.

PSALM 136 – Your Love Endures Forever

v1-3 I give thanks to you for are good, you are God of gods and LORD of lords Rev 19:16 – and your love endures forever.

v4-26 You are Creator v4-9, Rescuer v10-16 and Victor v17-22. v23-26 You are my Friend v23, Savior v24 and Provider v25. You are the God of Heaven, Maker and Keeper of all things v26.

PSALM 137 – I Consider You My Highest Joy

When the people of Judah went into exile in Babylon because of their rebellion and rejection of God they were filled with sorrow. We must contemplate the cause of our misfortunes and consider our highest joy v6; 126:1.

v1-3 Sometimes I sit and weep at how bad things are.

v4-9 Even then I will remember you – my highest joy v6.

PSALM 138 – On Bended Knees I Come

v1,2 I will praise you with all my heart. I will bow down before you because you have exalted above all things your name and your Word. Many problems and circumstances are due to ignoring God. The state of the nations is a result of denying his sovereignty and because people do not come on bended knees and do not honor the LORD and his Word.

v3 My fellowship with you makes me bold and stout hearted.

v4-8 You will fulfil your purpose for me – and the earth.

PSALM 139 – Search me, O God and Know My Heart

This is the personal revelation and expression of one who has come into an intimate relationship with God through a daily walk in his Presence. It is now open to all who will make the effort to commit to God and respond to the leading of the Holy Spirit 89:15-17. God is involved in every aspect of our existence.

v1-6 **You are all knowing** – omniscient. You know everything about me - even the thoughts of my mind v4. Your hand on my life is too wonderful for me to understand v5,6. There is nothing I can hide so I can be completely open with you Heb 4:13.

v7-12 **You are all present** – omnipresent. You are everywhere I go v7. You are always with me so there is nothing for me to fear v10; Jos 1:9; Mt 8:26. There is no darkness when I am with you for you are absolute light v11,12; Jn 1:7-9; 8:12; 1Jn 1:5.

v13-18 **You are all power** – omnipotent. You have control over my life and the universe. You created me, my amazing body, brain and soul, all worked out before the process began! You took part in every step of my existence and continue to do so v15,16. You even planned every day of my life v16.

I go to sleep in your Presence, pondering your thoughts – when I wake up you are still with me v17,18.

v19-22 **You are all holy** – separate from all limitation – absolute in all goodness. As you are holy – I would be too! Mt 5:48.

v23,24 **Search me, O God** Keep searching me, cleansing me and leading me in the Way – of eternal life 1Jn 5:11,12.

PSALM 140 – O LORD, You Are My God!

v1-5 Evil is all round me – violence, deceit, war, corruption, gossip, lies, hurts, traps, pride, self-centeredness.

v6-13 I say 'You are my God, my Sovereign LORD!' I know you uphold me, I live in your presence, praise your name v12,13.

PSALM 141 – My Prayer Rises to You

v1,2 I come to you quickly and regularly with my offering of prayer – like the evening sacrifice. My prayer rises before your Throne; you hear and command action Rev 5:8; 8:4.

v3-7 Do not let my heart be drawn to what is evil.

v8-10 My eyes are fixed on you, O Sovereign LORD.

PSALM 142 – Set Me Free to Worship You 1Sam 22:1-23

This psalm shows the magnitude of the circumstances as David fled from Saul and how he survived, rising above them. He considered he was in a prison and alone but still would not lay his hand against the LORD's anointed 1Sam 24;6; 26:9-11.

v1,2 I can come openly to you to express my heart and complain.

v3-6 It is you who knows my way, my refuge and my portion.

v7 I know you will set me free – to worship you Ex 3:12.

PSALM 143 – Your Good Spirit Leads Me
v1-4 Your faithfulness and righteousness are my relief – not my own goodness or ability Rom 3:9-26.

v5-6. I remember it is you I need, in the middle of all my trials.

v7-12 Teach me to lift up my soul to you v8, to hear your Holy Spirit and follow his leading and to do your will v10 gal 5:25.

PSALM 144 – It is You Who Gives Me Victory
v1,2 You prepare me to meet the day and train me through the circumstances of life to do whatever you require 2Tim 2:15,21.

v3,4 I am really insignificant in space and time - a breath, a shadow. And yet you think of me – you sent your Son to die for me so that I could have a relationship with you – for eternity!

v5 You part the heavens and come to my aid! Rev 1:4-6.

v9-15 I sing a new song for you give me victory Rev 5:9,10.

PSALM 145 – You Keep All Your Promises
v1,2 Every day I will exalt you and extol you forever.

v3-7 I meditate on your greatness, your power and your awesome works and commend you to my descendants.

v8-9 You are compassionate, slow to anger and rich in love.

v10-13 Your kingdom is everlasting and your dominion is forever. You are faithful to all your promises.

v14-21 You open your hand and satisfy the desires of all creatures v16. You are righteous in all your ways and near to all who call on you in truth, to lift them up v17,18.

PSALM 146 – The LORD Reigns, Forever
v1-6 You are my praise, help and hope, Maker of all things.

v7-10 You uphold the oppressed, feed the hungry, set prisoners free, give sight to the blind, lift up the discouraged, sustain the fatherless and frustrate the wicked. You reign forever, my God.

PSALM 147 – How Good it is to Praise You
v1,2 Praise the LORD - each prayer should begin with worship of who you are and thanksgiving for what you have done!

v3 You heal the broken-hearted and bind up my wounds.

v4 You determine the number of stars and call each of them by name! We cannot even see them all Job 38:31-33.

v5 Your power and understanding have no limit Is 55:8,9.

v6-10 You dwell with the humble and meek Is 57:15; Jas 4:6-10.

v11 You delight in me as I put my hope in you.

v12-20 I extol you for you have revealed your Word to me!

PSALM 148 – You have Raised Up the King!

v1-13 All creation praises you – it is your handiwork – the heavens v1-6 - the earth v7-10 - all people v11-12.

You alone are exalted in splendour above the creation v13.

v14 **You made Jesus the King** – foretold by the prophets; the strength and praise of your saints! Your saints are those who are close to your heart v14 – who acknowledged you and put their faith in you throughout the generations 2Chr 6:40; Heb 11:39.

Also those who have acknowledged Jesus as Savior, LORD and King Lk 2:10,11; Phil 2:9-11.

PSALM 149 – You are the Glory of the Saints

v1-3 I will sing a new song, rejoice, be glad, dance before you.

v4-5 You take delight in me! You have granted me salvation! This is a great honor in which I rejoice and sing for joy!

v6-9 Praise is like a two edged sword in my hands. With praise I defeat the accuser and carry out your judgement 8:2.

This is why there is so much praise in the Psalms. Our lives should be filled with praise so we will live effective and victorious lives. This is my glory! v9.

PSALM 150 – Let All with Breath Praise You – Amen!

v1 Praise God wherever you are – in his Presence! Praise him because of who he is - powerful and surpassingly great.

v2 Praise him for what he has done and will do for us.

v3-5 Praise him with everything you have and are.

v6 One day every creature will praise him – in his Presence.

The end of Psalms - **HALLELU YAH – PRAISE the LORD!**

Language of Prayer

The Psalms are primarily about communication with God. There are many expressions that assist in focusing our minds and developing our conversation. They may be used as steps into His Presence in your daily walk -

THANKSGIVING – to express gratitude; to appreciate; to love; to thank; be glad, joyful -
- give thanks to the LORD 1Chr 16:8; in all circumstances 1Thes 5:16-18
- sing and make music in your heart to the LORD Eph 5:18-20

PRAISE – to acknowledge worth - to express admiration - to enjoy God - to express how we feel towards Him - to extol His worth - to bless, rejoice, delight, sing, shout, dance and be joyful
- sing and make music in your heart to the LORD Eph 5:18-20
- sing praise to Him - declare His glory 1Chr 16:9-12
- as a royal priesthood to declare praises of Him 1Pet 2:9

CONFESSION – to be sorry for, to express regret – to come into agreement with God Ps 38:18 -
- against you have I sinned Ps 51:1-17; Father I have sinned against heaven and against you Lk 15:18,19
- if we say we have no sin we deceive ourselves 1Jn 1:8-10

PENITENCE – to express remorse; to repent; to turn away -
- he sat down, wept, mourned, fasted and prayed Neh 1:4
- have mercy on me, blot out my transgressions Ps 51:1-17

PETITION – to request; continue to ask; to be persistent; determined – to ask, plead, cry, seek mercy -
- hear from your dwelling place and forgive 2Chr 6:19-21; consider my sighs, I wait in expectation Ps 5:1-3
- everyone who asks receives Lk 11:9-10; he was heard because of reverent submission Heb 5:7

GUIDANCE – to wait for direction, comfort, strength to go on -
- trust, acknowledge – He will direct your path Pro 3:5-6
- come to me and I will give you rest Mt 6:33

WORSHIP – to show honor to; to regard as the highest object; to kiss towards; to acknowledge who God is; to express one's love and devotion – to adore, exalt, uplift, magnify, glorify, extol
- my LORD and my God Jn 20:28

ADORATION – to honor greatly, regard with the utmost esteem
- there is no one holy like the LORD 1Sam 2:2
- splendor and majesty, strength and joy 1Chr 16:27

CONSECRATION – to set aside for a special purpose (for God) – to offer, give up, submit, surrender -
- present your bodies, renew your minds – a sacrifice acceptable to God Rom 12:1-2

INTERCESSION – to plead for another; to stand in the place of
- I will not fail to pray for you 1Sam 12:03; I looked for one who would stand (and found none) Ez 22:20

MEDITATION – to share; commune; talk with; to experience -
- I consider your ways Ps 119:15; day and night Jos 1:8

WAIT UPON – rest, in anticipation, expectation, refreshment -
- be still before the LORD Ps 37:6; and know that I am God Ps 46:10; here I am. Send me Is 6:1-9
- speak LORD, your servant is listening 1Sam 3:10 - renew, soar, run, walk and not faint Is 40:31
- find rest, my soul Ps 62:5

COMMUNION – fellowship with; to enjoy -
- delight yourself in the LORD Ps 37:4; our fellowship is with the Father and His Son 1Jn 1:3,4
- earnestly I seek you, in the sanctuary, and behold your glory – my soul clings to you Ps 63:1-8
- I in them and You in Me Jn 17:3; ask what you will Jn 15:5-8

Examples of Prayer –
- The LORD's Prayer – Mt 6:9-13
- Temple dedication - 1Chr 16:7-36
- David's Confession – Ps 51
- David's love for God's Word – Ps 119
- Prayer for other Christians – Eph 1:15-21; 3:14-19

The Heavenly Realms – the spiritual dimension – where we are seated with Christ Eph 2:6
- We can pray in the Spirit – Jn 4:23. We have all spiritual blessings Eph 2:6
- We can enter the Most Holy Place – Heb 9:8; 10:19-22
- The Spirit intercedes with us Rom 8:26,27. Our example in intercession is Jesus Heb 7:25
- We need to be equipped to fight in spiritual warfare Eph 6:10-18.

Messianic Psalms

Psalm	verse	description	reference
2	1-3	He is anointed King of kings	Phil 2:9-11; Rev 19:11-16
	7	Deity of the Son of God	Mt 3:17; Heb 1:5; 5:6
	8-12	He is King and Judge	Jn 5:22,27; Acts 2:36
8	2	Power given to the humble	Is 57:15; Mt 21:15,16
	4-6	Set the future of the believer	Ac 2:31-35; Phil 2:5-11; Heb 2:6-9
16	8-11	Resurrection	Acts 2:22,23; Heb 13:25;15:12-17
18	4-6	Death and resurrection	Mk 8:31; Lk 18:31-34
	49	Salvation for the nations	Mt 28:18-20
22	1	Crucifixion	Mt 27:46; 34-50
	6-8	Mocked	Mt 27:39,40; Lk 23:35-39
	14	All my bones out of joint	Jn 19:17
	16	Hands and feet pierced	Is 53:7; Lk 23:33; Jn 19:18; 20:24-28
	18	Cast lots for his clothing	Mt 27:35; Jn 19:23,24
	22	Elevated believers to family	Heb 2:12
31	5	Cry from the cross	Mt 27:46
34	20	Bones not broken	Jn 19:31-37
35	11	Accused by false witnesses	Mt 26:59,60; Mk 14:57
	19	Hated without cause	Jn 15:23-25
40	6-8	Sacrificial death	Heb 10:5-7
41	9	Betrayed by a friend	Lk 22:48; Jn 13:18,21
45	6,7	Your throne	Heb 1:8-9
50	3-6	Second coming	Mt 24:30,31
	23	Provides salvation	Jn 10:10; 11:25
68	18	Ascension	Lk 24:51; Eph 1:20,21; 4:8
69	4	Hated without reason	Jn 15:25
	9	Cleansed the Temple	Jn:2:13-17
	21	Offered vinegar to drink	Jn 19:28,29
72	10,11	Kings will pay homage	Mt 2:1-11
89	4	An eternal throne	Ac 13:23; Lk 1:32,33,69
	26,27	Father and Son	Jn 10:30,38
	29	An eternal throne	Mt 19:28
	45	Early death	Mt 16:21
102	23-28	His return for the saints	Heb 1:10-12
109	25	People shook their heads	Mt 27:39
110	1	LORD said to my Lord	Mt 22:44; Acts 2:32-36; 5:30,31
	4	Order of Melchizedek	Heb 5:5,6; 7:1,17
	5,6	Judgment of the nations	Jn 5:22-27
118	22,23	The stone rejected	Mt 21:33-44; Eph 2:20; 1Pet 2:6-8
	26,27	Triumphal entry	Mt 21:8-11
132	17,18	Descendant of David	Lk 1:31-33

Proverbs

Introduction – Solomon, son of David was king of Israel for forty years at the height of its prominence 970-930 BC. He was a prolific thinker who wrote 3,000 proverbs and composed 1,005 songs. His wisdom was legendary 1Kin 4:29-34. He had an encounter with the LORD at the beginning of his reign when he requested a *discerning heart to govern your people and to distinguish between right and wrong 1Kin 3:5-15.* This was granted, as well as wealth and honor. Despite his wisdom a greater than Solomon has come Mt 12:42.

There is much godly wisdom in the Proverbs. Most of the issues of life are considered with advice about the moral path to follow. The alternative is often shown for contrast. The consequences of actions are also indicated. There are basic truths about practical, down to earth matters in words we can well understand. The general acceptance of many of the statements by most people shows that there is a basic standard of right and wrong, good and bad inherent in all individuals - man is uniquely a moral being. It is likely that Solomon recorded the lessons he had learned from his father David and the instruction of the priests as well as what he learned from his own vast experience and God-given gift of wisdom. Many of the thoughts are random and indicate a collection compiled over a period – there are four groups.

Author – Many were written by Solomon. Other contributors are noted.

Period – Solomon's thoughts and those of others were collated possibly after he had completed his great building projects and before he wrote Ecclesiastics, a time of idle reflection and self-indulgence – around 940 BC.

Theme – The futility of life without meaning.

The purpose and philosophies of life are critically examined. The overriding conclusion is – *the fear of the LORD is the beginning of wisdom 1:7.*

The Proverbs are God-centered 1:7; 2:5; 25:2. Most of the truths are confirmed in the New Testament. They are primarily concerned with man's efforts to understand God's moral government of the world.

The Superior Nature of Mankind Despite the similarities in the physical structure of creatures, the human being is unique.

The Scriptures describe mankind as being

- Man is a rational being, able to understand events. He can compare similar happenings in the present and past and draw valid conclusions from them for the future – this is scientific knowledge 16:9; 21:5; 24:3-5; Rom 1:18-20
- Man has a basic moral code – we all know a degree of good and evil – it is written in our hearts Rom 2:14-16. God's moral order is understood by the willing 1:1-7; 14:34
- Man is a spiritual being – more than flesh and blood, with an inmost being – a soul and a spirit 20:27

All three of these attributes are unique and demand that the individual be accountability.

There is a purpose behind our existence There is a reason for our lives and we have responsibility both to know God and obey his laws and we will be held accountable for our actions 5:22,23; Mt 12:36,37. Many turn away from God and even reject his existence in order to avoid his absolute standard - the decision is not intellectual but moral Ps 2:1-3.

Special Features - Wisdom is personified in many passages. We are hearing directly from the Holy Spirit and the instruction is accompanied by a promise of God. We are invited to know God - to acknowledge him, trust him, honor him, listen to him, commit to him and he will direct us, bless us and cause our plans to succeed 1:23; 2:1; 3:5,6. It is possible to know God personally and to grow in that relationship daily Rev 3:20. It is sometimes stated that prosperity and long life follow the good, moral law-abiding and wise, whereas poverty, suffering and early death face the wicked. This is a superficial and optimistic view, yet the principle is sound. While we cannot completely know God's ways which are above us we can expect God's provision and protection when we commit our ways to him Rom 8:28-30.

Many of the statements in Proverbs are unrelated. A tabulation of some of the themes is provided (ref p82).

SUMMARY
Proverbs of God's Ways – 1:8 to 9:18 (these are anonymous)
Proverbs of Solomon – 10:1 to 22:16
Proverbs of the Wise – 22:17 to 24:22
Proverbs of Solomon – 25:1 to 29:27 (some in both sections)
Words of Agur 30:1-33
Words of King Lemuel 31:1-31

Statement of Purpose

1:1 The main author is stated to be Solomon and nothing is added to the content or value of the work by speculation. There is enough evidence to support his authorship.

1:2-6 The purpose of Proverbs is to provide wisdom and discipline, standards and guidance for living daily a prudent life.

1:7 The fear of the LORD is the beginning of wisdom v7 – this axiom is repeated three more times 2:5; 9:10; 15:33; also Ps 14:1; Is 33:5-6 - this is the foundation for a victorious and effective life.

Wisdom This is defined as having the power of judging properly what is true or right – having scholarly knowledge that assists understanding. Throughout the ages leaders have sought to develop systems based on the philosophies of mankind to provide stable societies. These have ranged from the concept of common good through rule of the people for the people to totalitarian dictatorships and extermination of dissenters. All have failed to produce peace, security and prosperity because of the frailty and uncontrolled corruption of human nature at all levels of society.

Many people seek to ignore or reject God and cast off constraint Ps 2:1-3. They think that they will benefit best by having perceived freedom of personal choice without the constraint of God's requirements. They abandon an absolute standard and seek to *be like God, knowing good and evil Gen 3:5*. While they accept that laws must be established, the desire of many is to determine morality by consensus. The variable standards between countries and societies show the difficulties of leaving the determination of justice to the powerful. Despite our best efforts the problems of fallen human nature continue to plague society unabated.

The Wisdom of God The Scriptures refer to wisdom as the knowledge of God, his world, and his ways for achieving the best for his creation. His wisdom also includes his moral standard of right and wrong and what is best for mankind Is 48:17. This absolute standard is based on his divine nature and character. His knowledge has been revealed as recorded in the Bible and most completely in the life, death and resurrection of his Son Jesus Christ.

Since the time of Jesus, the Western World has developed a means of government based on the Word of God. The Ten Commandments and ethics of the Bible have resulted in stability, a degree of equity and prosperity that has benefited the majority. Scientific understanding has grown considerably as a result of the belief in God and a universe of order which has led to unprecedented gains for the people.

The problems within the Christian era can be traced back to the failure of people in all walks of life to apply the principles of the Word of God. It is on this basis that the Book of Proverbs should be read and by which the most benefit will be achieved. The truths for good and bad are as relevant and applicable today as they were 3,000 years ago.

1. Proverbs of God's Ways – Chapters 1:8 to 9:18 (these are anonymous)
The Benefits of Following God's Ways

1:8-19 **Hold on to your beliefs** Remember the advice of parents v8,9. Do not be led astray by others, from what you know is right. There is pressure from commercialism, popular opinion and alternative standards to conform Gen 3:6. Departure from principles leads to disappointment and regret.

1:20-32 **Rejecting God's Wisdom** Here wisdom is personified as the Holy Spirit - calling to us, seeking our response 20,21. One of the reasons for rejecting God is not science or logic - it is the desire for independence - to live with minimum restraint v24. People blame God when things go wrong and he does not answer them - but they have not recognized him or responded to his direction and ways v28-31.

God's offer of his plan of salvation is inferred – *if you had responded to my rebuke I would have poured out my heart to you v23* – this actually took place on the cross of Calvary Jn3:16. The consequence of rejecting God's goodness is also to be expected v24-32.

1:33 **Responding to God** His promise is sure - *but whoever listens to me will live in safety and be at ease without fear of harm.* Freedom from anxiety is the promise of Jesus and is the experience of those who put their trust in him Mt 6:25,33; 11:28-30. Trust is not token belief but genuine commitment 3:5,6.

2:1-22 **God's Wisdom** To understand God's wisdom we must consider his Word -

• we must read it regularly, listening to God speak v1; 8:33,34

• we need to store it up – revising it, memorizing it and meditating on it v1; Jos 1:8

• we must apply it, genuinely, in our hearts and to our lives and situations v2; Heb 4:12,13

- we must ask for insight in prayer and through the Holy Spirit v3 who continues to guide those who obey him Acts 5:32
- we must search for wisdom as hidden treasure, of great worth v4; 25:2; Ps 119:14,162.

2:9 Then you will understand what is right and just and fair – every good path.

God's wisdom is given *generously to all without finding fault Jas 1:6.* The condition is that we must be prepared to believe it, not doubting, or we cannot expect to receive Jas 1:6-8.

Even those who profess belief in God neglect the regular reading and application of the Word of God to their peril - it contains all we need for salvation, for full and victorious life and for effective witnessing 2Tim 3:16,17.

2:10-22 The wisdom of God's Word will enter your heart to guide you in every situation and will keep you from harmful worldly activities and from evil people.

3:1-35 How do we apply God's wisdom?

First you must trust in the LORD with all your heart. Then you need to allow his instruction to take precedence over you own ideas. If you do acknowledge him in all your ways then he will make your paths straight – he will direct you v5,6; Rom 12:1,2.

As a result you will find the following blessings will flow -
- you can expect long life and prosperity v2
- you will experience good relationships v3
- you will find favor in the sight of God and man v4
- absolute trust and faith in God will cause your paths to be straight v5,6
- humility, reverence and commitment to God's ways will bring health to your body and nourishment of your bones! v7,8
- by honoring God in putting him first in all things you will know his provision in all things you need in life v9,10; Mt 6:33
- you will know his discipline and rebuke as part of the development of your character - it should be embraced as such – as you become more like Christ v11,12; Jas 1:2-4; 2Cor 3:16-18
- when you recognize that there is a fundamental wisdom and moral order by which God created the universe and follow it then this will guide you in your daily live to give long life, riches, honor, pleasant ways and a path of peace v13-20

- following God's ways will mean you are freed from anxiety and fear - you will have security, you will lie down in sweet sleep and your home will be blessed v21-35.

***3:19,20* The Laws of Nature** A fundamental principle of all science is that the universe is possible of being understood by the human mind. It is this belief that advanced science in the western world. Yet this premise cannot be derived from the universe – why should this be? The presence of the many laws by which the universe exists and functions and have been present from the first moment of creation has no natural explanation except - that is the way it is! The many constants that dictate the form and continuity of the world have no known derivation – they are like they are! The Bible record consistently reveals that the God, in whose image we have been created, caused it to be so 8:22-31; Job 38:33; Heb 11:3.

***4:1-17* God's Wisdom is vital** There are many choices in life. The importance of obtaining and holding, retaining and applying God's wisdom is emphasized - *it is your life v4,13*. Many have taken their own paths and lived to regret it v14-17.

***4:18,19* The path of the righteous** – means to have 'right standing with God' – to be without blame.
No one is righteous by their own deeds Rom 3:10-12; Is 64:6 - this is the problem for those who ignore God. Yet there is a righteousness from God, available by faith in Jesus Christ from first to last - which brings the believer into relationship with God where all of God's promises apply Rom 1:17; 3:21,22.

***4:20-22* God's Word is vital to our relationship with him** This means that the Bible must become part of our daily guidance and instruction. As we pay attention to his Word and spend time in his Presence he speaks to us, directs us and provides an abundant life and a healthy body Jn 10:10.

***4:23* The heart is the wellspring of life** The heart is seen as the seat of emotions. What is in the heart, the seat of our emotions, affects every area of life. It determines our attitudes, our focus and our motivation.

***4:24-27* Set your minds on things above** The key to victorious living is the direction of our gaze v25. Our focus determines our interest and the path we will follow. We must put away things we know to be wrong and focus on what we know to be right Col 3;1-4.

***5:1-14* Warning against the perils of adultery** Immorality is a path that leads to deception and loss, disappointment and ruin. It involves the breaking of one's covenant with the LORD for which the individual will be held accountable Mal 2:15,16.

5:15-20 The blessings of a secure marriage. God ordained the sanctity of marriage as the natural union between a man and woman for mutual support and godly procreation Gen 2:20-25. The importance of the instruction of the father and the mother in providing a balanced upbringing of children is emphasized 1:8. He blesses the home of the righteous 3:33. Infidelity breaks the bond of trust and unity within the whole family.

Human desires to hate discipline and spurn correction lead ultimately to ruin v12-14.

5:21-23 *A man's ways are in full view of the LORD and he examines all his paths* God is omnipresent - present in all places. He is omniscient – knowing all things Ps 139:1-16. Though difficult to comprehend by the finite mind this attribute applies to the good and bad. It is this characteristic that allows a personal relationship through the indwelling presence of the Holy Spirit. It is also the means by which God will call the individual to account Dan 7:9,10; Rev 20:11-15.

6:1-15 Foolish activities Warning against risk-taking v1-5, laziness v6-11 and plotting evil v12-15.

6:16-19 Foolish actions Seven things that the LORD hates – proud arrogance, lying, bloodshed, evil intent and action, false witness and discord.

6:20-35 Deceit of adultery Listen to good advice before the event. Immorality is deceptive in what it appears to offer and what it actually delivers. It leads to disgrace, jealousy and irreversible enmity. The one loved becomes the one despised. There is great suffering and hardship for the one who is deserted especially if children are involved.

7:1-27 Lust of adultery Further warnings of the consequences of adultery - temptation is driven by the eyes, flesh and heart – for a moment of empty pleasure the result is loss of reputation and death, of trust, relationship and self-respect.

8:1-14 *Does not wisdom call out?* God calls to us daily through the still small voice of the Holy Spirit – we only need to listen for him 1Kin 19:12. Often we choose to ignore him.

8:15,16 *By me kings reign and rulers make laws that are just* – this is the confidence we have when we pray for our leaders for they are responsible to God. All authority is in his hand and will be required to give account Is 40:23; Dan 2:21; 4:17.

***8:17-21* God's love and favor, provision and Presence** These are better than the riches of the world Mk 8:36,37.

***8:22-31* God is Creator of the Universe** God's wisdom was appointed from eternity, from the beginning, before the world began v23. The Scriptures have declared the finite nature of the universe from the very first records Gen 1:1; Job 38:4; Ps 33:6; 90:2; Pro 3:19; Is 40:26; 42:5; 45:12,18; Jer 10:12; Jn 1:1-3; Acts 17:24. The 'big bang theory' was reluctantly accepted by science over the 'steady state universe model' in the 1960's.

God's very first deed in creation was to supply the total energy from which matter and all things physical formed v22; Heb 11:3 – everything came from nothing!

God made the 'dust of the world' - the 'energy particles' from the first few minutes of creation that are common to all physical matter! v26; Gen 3:19.

It is only since the early 20th century that science has been able to confirm these facts regarding energy and matter within the standard big bang model of the universe.

It was the wisdom of God that brought into being the laws of nature that allowed the universe to form and be sustained. It was his wisdom that incorporated the many finely-tuned physical cosmological constants in the first moment of creation that allowed the universe to proceed and that currently control the existence of all things 3:19,20; Job 38:33.

Some ask 'Who made God?' This assumes a finite, physical deity. The God of Scripture is eternal, Spirit, who is self-existent v23 and must be sought in spirit and in truth Jn 4:24.

The mystery of the Trinity can be seen in this passage –

• the LORD who set the heavens in place v27

• the craftsman at his side v30 - Jesus Christ *in whom are hidden all the treasures of wisdom and knowledge Col 2:3. By him all things were created – in him all things hold together Col 1:16,17.* Also compare Jn 1:1,2; and Heb 1:2

• the Holy Spirit, appointed before the world began v 23 – hovering over the waters Gen 1:2.

***8:32-36* The Favor of the LORD** How do we find God's direction in our daily lives?

We come into his Presence each day and wait at the doorway, watching for him to speak. This picture v33-35 describes the quiet time of devotion that each of us needs to have – a special time each day when we wait on the LORD. We pray, worship, give thanks and let him know our heart. We read his Word and meditate on it before him. We listen to him and act on what he tells us. God will be found by those who take the time to watch and wait on him daily - then we will find life and know his favor. Those who are too busy to seek the LORD miss out on the blessing that comes from learning to walk in his Presence v36; Ps 89:14-17; Is 40:27-31.

9:1-6 **An invitation to seek God** through the Holy Spirit and dwell in his Presence Ps 91:1-2.

9:7-9 There are those who accept wisdom and become wiser - those who reject wisdom and mock. People tend to mock what they do not accept or understand.

9:10-12 ***The fear of the LORD is the beginning of wisdom and knowledge of the Holy One is understanding*** God is both knowable and necessary to give meaning and direction to life and eternity Jn 1:12,13.

9:13-18 **Who's call do you follow?** As there is One who calls us to greatness, so there is the call to self-seeking and wrongdoing that leads to destruction Eph 2:1-5.

2. Proverbs of Solomon – Chapters 10:1 to 22:16

10:1-32 **Two paths to follow** The alternatives are set before us – each verse bears consideration and requires a decision. Advice is given on morals, work, conversation, relationships, investment and most areas of life. God's ways lead to life, blessing and provision but those who do evil, their fears overtake them v24.

11:1-31 **A choice of conduct** Honesty, humility, integrity, righteousness and generosity reap a sure reward – evil comes to the one who searches for it. Be sure that the wicked will be punished v21. He who wins souls is wise v30.

12:1-28 **Righteousness** is the way of life and the path of immortality v28. Direction in right way is given.
While holy living is our aim there is a righteousness that comes through faith in Jesus from first to last Rom 1:17.

13:1-25 **Discipline is necessary** for us to grow intellectually, physically, morally and spiritually. This is a universal law 29:1.
He who gathers money little by little makes it grow v13.

14:1-35 **God's ways are best** for man v12, for his health v30 and for his family v26; Is 48:17.

14:34 **God's ways exalt a nation** - the ways of human nature lead to sin and disgrace. We see this around the world.

15:1-33 **God sees all things** – the wicked and the good v3. Prayer pleases him v8. The heart at peace with God brings joy to the whole being and health to the body v13, 30. Anxiety crushes the spirit v13. The LORD dwells with the humble v33.

16:1-33 **God directs all things** - All our plans and desires should be brought to the LORD for he brings success v1-9. Honesty and integrity are recognized v10-24. Our plans without God often end in disaster v25; 19:21. We may think we are in control *but its every decision is from the LORD v33.*

17:1-28 **Relationships** Guidelines on how to develop genuine friendships that continue at all times! v17.

17:22 **A Joyful Heart** A cheerful heart brings health like a medicine - bitterness dries the bones 15:13,30. Knowing Jesus brings this joy Jn 15:11.

18:1-24 **Friendship** What is the mark of friendship? Have many acquaintances – but there is a friend who sticks closer than a brother. Such a friend is of great worth and must be encouraged. Jesus is such a friend! Jn 15:14,15.

19:1-29 **General Wisdom** Many are angry with God and blame him for their misfortune, but do not acknowledge him in the good times v3. Kindness pleases God v17. Discipline is necessary for good conduct and character v18; 29:1.
Despite the plans in our hearts God's purpose prevails v21.

20:1-30 **God's Purposes Prevail** We need to search our intentions and motives v5. Learn from observation, think before you leap v12. Make plans and seek guidance in all areas of life v18. We cannot find what is best for us on our own because it is God who directs our steps v24. He searches our innermost being v27; 14:12; 16:1,3,9,25; 19:21; 21: Jer 10:23.

21:1-31 **No plan ultimately succeeds without God** Our ideas and plans may seem right to our understanding but God weighs the heart v2,30,31.

3. Proverbs of the Wise – Chapters 22:17 to 24:22

22:1-5 Humility, modest ambitions and generosity please God.

22:6-15 **Training and discipline** are necessary and of great benefit 13:24; 19:18; 23:13,14; 29:15. Without an appreciation of discipline as a child, a person is not properly equipped to face life and is less likely to succeed 29:1.

22:16-29 Integrity, honesty and skill are pleasing to God

23:1-24 Guidelines for being zealous for God v17.

24:1-34 Look out for the interest of others and those who are tempted v11. Get up after each time you fall v16.

4. Proverbs of Solomon – Chapters 25:1 to 29:27 (some are in both sections)

25:1-28 **The glory of mankind** God hides his wisdom so that we will search it out v2. Then we will prosper in all areas of life.
Diligence and refining produce quality v5.
Show the love of God in all areas of life v21,22.

26:1-28 Guidance against foolishness.

27:1-27 One cannot know what the future holds v1. Pursue humility and sound principles of life.
Strong friendships promote character v17.
Do not be led by desire, it is never satisfied v20.

28:1-28 **Admit faults** Obey the law v1-12. Confess and renounce sin and find forgiveness v13; Ps 51:1-19; 1Jn 2:1.

29:1-27 **Discipline brings wisdom** Human nature requires laws and the rod of correction. This is explained by the Fall and original sin Gen 3:22-24. In all societies restriction of behavior is mandatory. Discipline is essential for development in all areas of human endeavor v15,17; 10:17; 12:1; 19:18; 22:6,15; 23:13,14.

29:18-24 **Independence from God** Without a revelation - a standard, vision or plan of action - people cast off restraint. This is the appeal of natural science and biological evolution – there is a perceived excuse for turning away from God and his moral laws. The decision is not intellectual but moral.
We need God's discipline, his standard and his justice v26. This applies to the individual and the nation and is lacking around the world as revealed in corruption, domination and conflict.

29:25-27 **Eternal destiny** The ultimate need for faith in God relates to the finite nature of mankind. The natural science future for the soul is oblivion. God offers eternal life through faith in Jesus Mt 10:28; 16:26; Jn 3:16-18.

5. Words of Agur Chapter 30:1-33
This small collection of sayings contains amazing revelation about the Person and nature of God and of his Son Jesus.

30:1-3 **Knowledge of the Holy One** Humility and reverence are the approach to knowledge and relationship with God Is 57:15. We would not have detailed understanding of God and of his plan for mankind without his revelation through his Word and the coming of Jesus to earth.

30:4 **The Messiah** There is prophetic reference to the One who came down from heaven to be our Saviour and then ascended into heaven to be our Advocate. The Messiah is here spoken of as a Person and Son distinct from the Father. Jesus used this text in reference to himself as the Son of God Jn 3:13. Paul also used it in referring to Jesus Eph 4:8-10. The ultimate knowledge of God came through the life, death and resurrection of Jesus. He came to show us the Father. He removed the offense of sin so that the believer may come into eternal relationship with the Holy One v3.

30:5,6 **Every Word of God is flawless** – we can add nothing to it, or take anything away Ps 119:89. Jesus confirmed that every smallest dot and least stroke must be fulfilled Mt 5:17,18. The warning against adding to or taking away from God's Word is repeated v6; Rev 22:18,19.
Many have changed or added to God's Word and so have come under this penalty. It is significant that those who deny Jesus as the Son of God seek to refute God's Word.

30:7-9 **A contented life** There are many things we want in life *but godliness with contentment is great gain 2Tim 6:6*. It is good to learn the secret of contentment Phil 4:11-13.

30:10-17 **Negative actions** Self-centered attitudes hurts those around us and eventually destroy us.

30:18-33 **Learn from observation** We may learn many things from life around us. Better to gain wisdom from life and the experience of others than to suffer repeatedly. Some things are difficult to understand v18-20, some are to be avoided v21-23, some reveal wisdom v24-31 and conflict is to be harmful v32,33.

6. Words of King Lemuel Chapter 31:1-31
31:1-7 **Indulgence** Spending time and resource on fleeting pleasure brings no gain. Control feelings and act responsibility.

31:8,9 **Integrity** We must all show justice and act on behalf of those who are unable to help themselves.

31:10-31 A Wife of Noble Character The importance of the wife and mother in the family is described -

• The marriage and family relationship were instituted by God at the beginning for complementary support and union of the male and female. This relationship is also required for procreation and balanced upbringing of children Gen 1:27,28

• Man was created with the need for relationship and dependence - no helper suitable was found

• Woman was created as a helpmate and coworker, perfectly complementing Gen 2:20-24 – give her the recognition and reward she has earned v31

• There are corresponding responsibilities for the husband and wife that provide the marriage bond – principally to submit to one another out of reverence for Christ Eph 5:21-33.

An understanding of this institution of marriage and commitment to it is fundamental to all societies and to successful families.

Themes in Proverbs

	Theme	ref	Text	other references
1	Accountability	15:11	death lies open before the hearts of men	11:5,7; 14:32
2	Anxiety	12:25	an anxious heart weighs a man down	1:33; 10:24
3	Adultery	5:1-23	I have come to the brink of ruin	2:16-19; 6:20-35; 7:1-2
4	Blessing	10:24	what the righteous desire will be granted	8:32-36; 10:6,7,22
5	Children	1:8,9	listen to your father - your mother	4:1-9;10:1; 6:20; 13:1,2
		22:6	train a child - he will not turn from it	22:15; 23:13,14; 29:15-1
6	Character	3:3,4	let love and faithfulness never leave you	4:25-27; 8:12-14; 10:6,
7	Conversation	10:18-21	the lips of the righteous nourish many	4:24; 10:11-14; 28:23
		12:14	from the fruit of his lips he is filled	12:17-23; 13:2,3; 14:3
		16:23,24	a wise man's heart guides his mouth	18:13,20,21
		18:7	a fool's mouth is his undoing	18:2,6
8	Creation	3:19,20	laid the earth's foundations - set the heavens	
		8:26	before he made - the dust of the world	8:22-31
		22:2	the LORD is the Maker of them all	
9	Discipline	3:11,12	the Lord loves you - as a Father	12:1; 19:18; 23:13,14
		27:21	man is tested by the praise he receives	1:7; 5:22,23; 10:17
10	Evil intent	6:12-15	disaster will overtake him in an instant	9:13-18; 16:29,30
		6:16-19	these things the LORD hates	
11	Family	3:33	the LORD blesses the home of the righteous	13:22
		31:10-31	the wife of noble character	5:15-19; 12:4; 14:1; 18:
12	Fear of the Lord	1:7	is the beginning of knowledge	2:5; 3:7; 9:10,11; 19:2
		8:13	is to hate evil	10:27; 14:2; 28:14
13	Foolishness	1:7	despise wisdom and discipline	9:13-18
		10:24	what the wicked dreads overtakes him	
14	Friendship	17:17	a friend loves at all times	18:24; 27:6,9,10
		27:17	iron sharpens iron, one man sharpens another	13:20
15	Generosity	3:27,28	do not withhold good from those who deserve	
		11:24,25	one gives freely, yet gains even more	19:17; 21:13; 22:9
		19:17	he who is kind to the poor lends to the LORD	25:21,22; 28:27
16	God sees	5:21-23	a man's ways are in full view of the LORD	20:27
		15:3	the eyes of the LORD are everywhere	
17	Gossip	11:12,13	betrays confidence - keep a secret	16:27,28; 18:8; 26:20-2
18	Guidance	2:1-9	you will understand - every good path	4:10-17; 11:14
19	Health	3:7,8	fear the Lord and shun evil	
		4:20-23	health to your body - the wellspring of life	14:30; 15:13; 30; 17:2
20	Humility	3:34,35	the LORD gives grace to the humble	
		11:2	pride brings disgrace, humility brings wisdom	15:33; 25:6,7,27; 27:1,
21	Independence	14:12	in the end it leads to death	16:1-4,9,25; 21:2-5
		19:3,21	a man's own folly ruins his life	
		29:18	no revelation - the people cast off constraint	
22	Investment	13:11	gathers money little by little makes it grow	6:1-5; 21:5

Theme	ref	Text	other references
Judgment	16:5	evil will not go unpunished	2:21,22; 8:36; 11:7,8
	24:11,12	there will be no excuse	11:21,23,31
Law of the LORD	3:1,2	will prolong your life - bring you prosperity	30:5,6
	29:18	blessed is he who keeps the law	6:20-23; 7:1-4; 28:9
Listen to the LORD	1:33	lve in safety, without fear of harm	2;1-5
Love	10:12	covers over all wrongs	3:3,4
Majesty of God	30:2-4	what is his name and the name of his son	
Peer pressure	1:10-19	do not give in to them	2:12-15,20-22
Plans	16:1-4;9	Commit your plans to the LORD	20:18; 21:2-5,31
	19:21	but it is the LORD' purpose that prevails	
	20:24	a man's steps are directed b the LORD	
Prayer	15:8	the prayer of the upright pleases the LORD	8:15,16
Pride	11:2	when pride comes, then comes disgrace	
Prosperity	3:9,10	honor the Lord with your wealth	15:16
	10:22	the blessing of the LORD brings wealth	8:17-21
Repentance	28:13	whoever renounces sin finds mercy	
Righteousness	11:30	the fruit of righteousness is a tree of life	10:2,16,24-32; 15:26
	14:34	righteousness exalts a nation	11:5,14; 28:4,5
	18:10	the name is a strong tower - run nto it	10:27
	24:16	though he falls he will rise again	21:2,3
Salvation	1:23,24	if you had resonded - you have rejected me	1:23-33; 11:4,19,20; 20:9
	16:6	through love and faithfulness sin is atoned	12:28;14:32; 29:26
Satisfaction	27:20	never satisfied - are the eyes of man	30:15,16
Sin	14:9	fools mock - good will is found in the upright	6:12-15,16-19; 13:21
Soul-winner	11:30	he who wins souls is wise	
Sovereignty	8:15,16	by me kings reign - by me princes govern	21:30,31; 27:1
	16:33	every decision is from the LORD	16:4,9
	20:24	a man's steps are directed by the LORD	
Sweet sleep	3:21-24	preserve sound judgement and discernment	
Trust in the Lord	3:5-7	he will make your paths straight	29:25
	3:25,26	have no fear of sudden disaster	
	23:17,18	there is surely a future hope for you	
Wisdom	8:1-11	to you O men, I call out, choose my instruction	8:12-36
	8:22,23	I was appointed from eternity	24:3-7
Wisdom for life	1:1-7	discipline and understanding for a prudent life	7:1-4; 14:8
Wise ways	10:29	a refuge for the righteous	6:1-19
	30:24-28	wisdom from small things	
Word of God	2:5	you will find the knowledge of God	2:1-11
	4:20-23	they are life - and healing to your whole body	
	8:32-36	listen to my instruction - watching daily	22:17-21
	25:2	it is the glory of kings to search out a matter	
	30:5	every word of God is flawless	
Work ethic	6:6-11	how long will you lie there, you sluggard	10:4,5; 12:27; 13:4
	18:9	one who is slack in his work - destroys	

Ecclesiastes – preacher

Introduction – Ecclesiastes contains fine poetry and profound truths. However many of the observations come from a person who has lost their relationship with God and is only living a form of religion.

The Book causes us to ask – what is the meaning of life – the purpose for our existence? To consider that the brief term of human life on earth comes from nothing and ends in nothing beyond death is indeed emptiness.

Mankind was made above beast with intellect, reason and the need to seek answers to life and surroundings. We have God's 'image' in us Gen 1:26,27; 2:7. To seek and find the God of our creation and his plan for each of us is our prime purpose in life Jer 29:11-13 - both in this life and the next.

Author – The Book fits Solomon – the wisest fool - written around 935 BC. He was well placed to explore by wisdom all that is done under heaven 1:12,13. Solomon had the resources – he was wise, rich, famous, a prolific builder and did spend much time in studying life 1Kin 4:29-34. Initially he was loved by the LORD 2Sam 12:25.

Solomon's Fame At the beginning of his reign Solomon was a good king. He asked God for wisdom which he received and he experienced two great moments when God appeared to him 1Kin 3:5. He was the wisest man till Jesus Christ Mt 12:42.

Solomon was known for his legendary wisdom, immense wealth and enormous influence. His kingdom extended from the Euphrates River to Egypt Jos 1:4; 1Kin 10:24; 2Chr 9:22-26. He became king at 19 years of age and spent the first twenty-five years of his reign building the Temple and his palace as well as many other great construction projects.

Solomon's Folly However in the last ten years Solomon turned away from the LORD drawn by his foreign wives.

He incurred the anger of the LORD and the ten northern tribes of Israel were lost within a week of his death 1Kin 11:1-13.

He died a foolish king at the age of 59.

He ignored the instructions of God for a king -

• write the Law on a scroll, read it and learn to revere the LORD Deu 17:18

• do not accumulate large amounts of wealth Deu 17:17; 1Kin 10:23

• do not accumulated horses from Egypt Deu 17:16; 1Kin 10:28

- do not take many foreign wives Deu 17:17; 1Kin 11:1-3
- do not worship other gods 1Kin 11:4-6.

Solomon's Example We must learn from Solomon - success, position and status lead to pride and self-confidence which must be dealt with before God. Compromise and lack of discipline (departing from the Word of God) result in ultimate downfall.

Period - It is possible that in the idle years after his building program around the age of 50 Solomon began his philosophical investigation into the meaning of life and wrote Ecclesiastes as he drifted away from God. Some critics claim the author was not Solomon due to apparent language difference between 200 and 900 BC. They claim it was written by an unknown person around 250 BC who put himself in the shoes of the aging apostate king. This does not add to or subtract from the value of the text and the wisdom and directions it provides for our lives today.

Theme - The conclusion of the Book provides the result of the study - *Fear God and keep his commandments for this is the whole duty of man – for God will bring every deed into judgment including every hidden thing, whether it is good or evil 12:13,14; Micah 6:8.*
The writer had a good general knowledge of God and the ways of the world. However despite all his wisdom he could not understand God's working. Knowledge of the LORD is lacking compared with the Psalms of David. There is no evidence of a relationship with God.
He dealt with the vanity of worldly wisdom and striving. Human philosophy of life is flawed. All that man can derive from thought and experience without the revelation from God leads to life without meaning. There is a repudiation of all human wisdom, however great, where the fear of God is lacking. Man may discover much about God and life but his research only has substance if it is carried out in the fear and respect of the LORD. The fundamental lesson is to have reverent fear of God and keep his commandments.

Special Features - Like all Books of the Bible Ecclesiastes was inspired! So we can benefit much by detailed study. However we would not agree with many of the observations due to our relationship with God through Jesus and our knowledge of his overall Word. It is important to check each point against the New Testament which provides a greater revelation of the Person and nature of God. Many of the frustrations of Ecclesiastes are answered by the life and teaching of Jesus.

The Pursuit of Life

1:1 Solomon, son of David, King of Jerusalem – his purpose and conclusions are recorded.

1:2,3 **What is the Purpose of Life** In later years Solomon explored life – what is the result of all our effort? Many who have everything in life give up - even take their own life! The conclusion is – it is meaningless! All that man seeks after for satisfaction results in vanity and shallow pride that brings emptiness and despair.

1:4-7 **The Repetitive Cycle** The universe continues independent of our efforts. That the wind, air and sea currents follow definite cycles essential to life on earth was not understood in the day of Solomon v6, nor the evaporative water cycle v7.

1:8-10 **No satisfaction in human effort** There is no remembrance of what we have done. Life is a cycle of repetitive acts; nothing is new or remembered v9-11.

1:12-18 **Worldly Wisdom** Solomon devoted himself to explore knowledge, science, the arts – he even pursued foolishness, searching for meaning. He concluded that there was no satisfaction, only sorrow and grief, futility, frustration and vexation (annoying) of spirit v17,18.

2:1-11 **Indulgence** He gave himself to pleasure, laughter, intoxication, sated desire, work, projects, possessions, wealth, music – these are the things all mankind strive for - the delights of the heart of man! v8. He denied himself nothing his eyes desired v10. Yet he decided everything was meaningless and led to emptiness. At the end of all toil and accomplishment there remains an unsatisfied desire for more v11; 6:3.

2:12-16 **Eternal Life** For the people of the world there is no hope. There is no difference in wisdom or foolishness for both the fool and the wise end in death!
We now know that Christ Jesus *has become for us wisdom from God - that is, our righteousness, holiness and redemption* 1Cor 1:20-25,29,30; 1Jn 5:11,12 The end of physical life for the believer is eternal life – graduation to fulfillment.

2:17-23 **Depression** People begin to hate life because of its meaninglessness - ***all his days his work is pain and grief; even at night his mind does not rest v23.*** This has been the lot of many in all generations from all walks of life and has led to alcohol, drugs and suicide even among the rich and famous. How different to the experience of those who have learned to put their trust in God 5:19,20; Ps 4:7,8.

2:24-26 Materialism – the theory that places all things in the universe in a material framework – this is the premise of natural science. Solomon considered living for oneself - to eat, drink and find satisfaction in work. This too is meaningless and leads to pessimism. *For without him* **(God)** *who can eat or find enjoyment? v25.*

3:1-22 Fatalism – the belief that all events are influenced by fate and therefore inevitable. Many people put this down to chance. The embodiment of this belief is the possibility that the universe happened by chance without a procuring cause.

3:1-10 Solomon recognized that everything happens to a plan outside our primary influence v1-8; Pro 16:9.

3:11-17 Everything is Beautiful God has made a beautiful world and put a longing for eternity in the heart of every person v11. Yet one cannot understand the purpose of life without a knowledge of God who has given each of us a gift – to live and find satisfaction in all our toil v13. Those who choose to ignore God can only seek to find some happiness while they can as we will each be called to account in the end v15,17.

3:13 The Gift of God It is a humbling experience to contemplate that each one of us had no say in our birth - our being, location, abilities, circumstances or our life expectancy. It is all a gift from God revealing his sovereignty and interest - *He himself gives all men life and breath and everything else - we are God's offspring Acts 17:24-29.* There is no room for pride!

3:18-20 Materialistic oblivion Solomon concluded there is no difference between man and beast – meaningless existence and return to the cosmic chemical cycle v19,20. This is the prediction of natural science and biological evolution.
The Bible confirms that man is superior to the physical world – made in the image of God and created for relationship with God with potential for eternal future Gen 1:26; Heb 2:5-8. The human being has a body, a soul and a spirit which must be regenerated by the Spirit of God Eph 1-5; Jn 1:12,13; 3:3-8.

3:20-22 Who knows if the spirit of man rises? Solomon found no hope beyond the grave.
We now have the assurance of eternal life through faith in Jesus who rose again from the dead as our example Jn 3:16; Rom 6:22,23; 1Cor 15:3-8.

***4:1-6* Oppression** Subjection of the masses is the resort of authority and is common place in organizations around the world from governments to families.

It is based on envy and covertness – the desire to possess, to control, in order to maintain power, when moral practices fail. Ultimately it is the oppressor that fails.

***4:7,8* Loneliness** To live for oneself without companionship and reliable dependencies is a miserable business. Inability and unwillingness to relate and contribute too often lead to regrettable and irretrievable circumstances.

***4:9-12* Relationship** Mankind was created with the need for community Gen 2:18,24. A team will always achieve more than the collective efforts of the individuals. Disunity detracts from all endeavors. Broken commitments lead to broken lives.

***4:13-16* Success** There is even no satisfaction in success by itself for it is transitory - after all the hard work one is forgotten and others reap the gain. Satisfaction is in the chase as well as the catch.

***5:1-7* God is in Heaven** Many have a concept of a physical heaven a long way off. They consider that God is remote and fearsome v1,2. Yet God is omnipresent - present in all places. Jesus taught us that God is personal and our Father and we can have an intimate relationship with him Jn 17:20-23. While we must always stand in awe of God we can approach him at any time Mt 6:9-13. It is best to have less to say and to keep our word v3-7.

***5:8-14* Wealth and Labor** Those who pursue wealth never have enough v10. They become bound by greed and are never satisfied 1Tim 6:9,10. Their burdens increase and so do their needs v11. The worker who learns to be satisfied with his labor finds rest v12.

***5:15-17* What does he gain?** We must remember we began with nothing and will certainly end with nothing but the record of our deeds and actions v15. Jesus taught this with the parable of the Rich Fool - *this very night your life will be demanded of you Lk 12:16-21.* We each have a night in store!

***5:18-20* The Secret of Contentment** If one finds the necessities of life and can be happy in work, this is a gift of God. An occupied person has gladness of heart – **this is the secret of contentment** – a secret that must be discovered, learned and put into practice Phil 4:11,12; 1Tim 6:6-8.

6:1-12 Enjoyment comes from God All things are worthless without the ability to enjoy them Neh 8:10. Who knows what is good for a man in life?

7:1-19 Philosophy The study of the principles underlying all knowledge and being, include natural, moral and metaphysical – but excluding the revelation (knowledge) of God who is Spirit. The wisdom of man is based on human intuition and experience which all comes from God – the good and the bad v14. Wisdom cannot discover the future v14. It is best to be conservative and be cautious of all extremes! v18.

7:20-29 Moral Order There is a problem with human nature – the presence of evil v20. There is a moral order in life and in the psychic of each individual – we know what is basically right and wrong. The feeling of guilt is difficult to ignore and often leads to emotional problems. Many ask 'why does God allow evil' – an admission of our inability to do what is right – when things go wrong for us it is the fault of God. That is why we need redemption. We cannot meet the absolute standard of God Rom 3:23; 6:23.

The common answer is to change or to ignore the standard. But this does not resolve the greater issue of death Pro 16:25; Heb 9:27. The Gospel is the only answer to the problem of sin and of death Jn 3:16.

7:29 *God made mankind upright but men have gone in search of many schemes*. How do we account for the tendency of each person to chose wrong under certain conditions? This is the consequence of original sin Gen 3:17,18. *The hearts of men moreover are full of evil and there is madness in their hearts while they live and afterward they join the dead 9:3.* It is the knowledge of this truth that leads one to the Savior 1Jn 2:1,2.

8:1-17 Look out for yourself – toe the line, keep out of trouble; enjoy life where you can - eat, drink and be glad Is 22:13. Jesus warned against this attitude in the parable of the Prodigal Son Lk 15:13.

9:1-18 Atheism - The futility of life without hope.
● All share a common destiny v1-3. This is a problem for many people today - the sense of being unable to change circumstances
● Physical life is the only knowledge v4-9. The physical world is the extent of human experience
● There are no Absolutes v10. There is no absolute God and no absolute moral code. Truth is subjective, so do want seems right to the best of your ability

- Time and chance happen to all v11,12. The universe came into existence by a random occurrence and so life is governed by chance
- Wisdom is the measure of the person v13-18. Mankind is at the center of the universe and may determine what is true – this is the ultimate arrogance of man before God.

Believers *know that in all things God works for the good of those who love him who have been called according to his purpose Rom 8:28.*

Jesus gives us hope, expectation - in this life Rom 15:13 and in the life after death Jn 14:1-4.

10:1-20 **Humanism** – life based on human effort or achievement. The ultimate offense to the Creator is to place humankind at the center of the universe. There is no absolute truth or moral value – rights are determined by the pursuit of consensus. The purpose of existence is to live life's brief sojourn well till summoned to deal with your invincible defeat. Without reason for life there is only resignation.

11:1-10 **Life resorts to chance without God** This conclusion has been reached by modern day science in the theory of Chaos - nothing is predictable with certainty! Many have a sense of credence in fortune - a 'harmless attraction' to the occult, condemned and forbidden by God Deu 18:10-13.

A Relationship with God

12:1-6 Remember your Creator in the days of your youth, before the days of trouble come – before it is too late and *the silver cord is severed v6.* Advice of older people who have suffered the consequences of wrong decisions in youth is precious guidance but often ignored.

12:7 **Theism** *The dust returns to the ground it came from and the spirit returns to God who gave it.* Solomon showed his godly upbringing Gen 2:7; 3:19. Science has discovered that our bodies are made from the same particles (atoms) that make up the rest of the universe – we are of the dust of the stars (and ground). However the Bible also states that the soul is immortal and that our eternal future will be governed by our acceptance of Jesus Christ as Savior and Lord Rev 20:11-15 – knowledge beyond the realm of physical science.

12:8 Everything is meaningless! **Nihilism** – the total lack of belief in religion or moral principles and duties in established laws and instructions. Many accept the conclusion of Solomon that life has no meaning but to enjoy, contribute and end in oblivion with no hope for eternity. For all his wisdom, study and searching out Solomon failed to follow his own advice and that of his father David from his youth – *show yourself a man and observe what the LORD your God requires 1Kin 2:1-3.* He forsook the wisdom he sought for the folly he despised 2:13.

The Conclusion of the Matter

Solomon's extensive research into the purpose and meaning of existence reveals the hopelessness of all philosophies of life that exclude the Eternal Creator God.

12:9-14 Fear God and keep his commandments for this is the whole duty of man – for God will bring every deed into judgment including every hidden thing, whether it is good or evil v13,14. This conclusion was reinforced by Jesus and the prophets Mt 22:37-40; Mic 6:8.

The born again believer has the expectation and certainty of eternal life Jn1:12; 1 Jn 5:11,12.

Song of Songs

Introduction – The Song of Songs is poetry about the beauty of human love between a king and a lowly country lass - a Shulamite from northern Galilee, taken to the royal court, perhaps the bride of his youth.

It can also be taken as an allegorical picture of God's love to Israel, to the church and to the individual believer. Spiritual blessing and motivation can be gained by studying it in this way. We may even see it as a parable – an earthly story which conveys and reinforces hidden spiritual truth. As it is the inspired Word of God it is our glory to search the matter out Pro 25:2. There are a number of references in Scripture to the marriage relationship in comparing our walk with the LORD. God is the husband of Israel Is 54:5. Jesus is the bridegroom Jn 3:29. The church is the bride Rev 19:7. The desire for deep intimacy with us was also expressed by Jesus Jn 15:11; 17:20-23.

Author – Solomon, king of Israel.

Period – During Solomon's reign from 970 to 930 BC

Theme - The marriage relationship is the ultimate human intimacy.

Beyond this is the intimacy of union with Christ - available to all believers. Paul described this union as a profound mystery Eph 5:32.

If we can look beyond the physical story to the spiritual relationship with our Lord through the indwelling presence of the Holy Spirit a deeper union with Christ will result - but only for those who take the time personally to seek, search, hunger and thirst for it. In this way we grow up into Christ Eph 4:15.

The key is - *I am my lover's and my lover is mine 2:16.*

We may see three parties – the LORD, oneself and believing friends.

The Joy of First Love

1:1-4 **The New 'Born Again' Believer** Our first love for Jesus was a great joy to us – we longed to be in the presence of our Savior, hungry for his Word, in prayer and in fellowship. There was a new awareness of sin from which we had been delivered.

Let the king bring me into his chambers v4 - we were so aware of the heavenly realm. This pleasure is available for all who genuinely seek it -

- *I have seen you in the sanctuary Ps 63:2*
- *Till I entered the sanctuary of God Ps 73:17*
- *My soul yearns, faints for the courts of the LORD Ps 84:1.*

1:5 A New Perspective We had a whole new worldview - eternity was opened to us - the old was gone, the new had come Col 1:13,14. We wanted to share our newfound relationship with others.

1:6 Distractions – Sadly that first love fades in many. The first joy begins to be crowded out by the world. We are not supported and counseled by believing friends - we become mediocre. Old attractions reappear - peer pressure, worldly friends and pursuits, drifting us away from the LORD.

We need to remember the height from which we have fallen! Repent and return to it and foster it through our regular 'Quiet Time' with him! Rev 2:4,5.

Quiet Time For the new believer the practice of setting aside time each day to read the Bible and pray is vital. While this can become a mechanical exercise, the main purpose is to develop a relationship with Jesus by being in his Presence. This experience then extends into the daily walk Eph 5:18-20.

Unfortunately, with time the practice diminishes and with it the 'first love'. All believers must take the example of new born babies and crave regular time in the Word and the Presence of Jesus if they are to continue to grow and be effective 1Pet 2:2.

1:7,8 The way back is by following the Shepherd How do we return to that intimacy of first love. We must ***follow the tracks of the sheep*** *v8* - those who are feeding from the Shepherd. It is by renewed Quiet Time and fellowship with him each day and with others who also want to grow.

There are five activities which are essential to growth –
- Prayer – don't be anxious about anything Phil 4:5-7
- Reading the Word – let the Word of Christ dwell in you richly Col 3:16
- Worship – give thanks in all circumstances 1Thes 5:16-19
- Fellowship - spur one another on to love and good works Heb 10:24,25
- Witnessing - we are Christ's ambassadors 2Cor 5:20

When these spiritual disciplines are exercised regularly the believer will grow in relationship with Jesus and develop in victorious and effective living 2:42-47; Col 2:6,7.

It is important to meet regularly in homes to practice these spiritual disciplines with other committed believers in the presence of Jesus Mt 18:19,20; 2Tim 2:2.

Return to the flock and your first love will return v7.

With perseverance you will become a shepherd as well, helping others to come to the LORD and grow v8.

Discipleship – Following Our Beloved!

***1:9-17* When we are in union with the LORD** we are used in his work – we carry his fragrance to others 2Cor 2:14-16. Our fellowship with him deepens, our love grows stronger and our faith becomes secure v15-17.

2:1-7 Mutual Affection

- **We are like a beautiful flower to Jesus** - a lily among thorns
- **Jesus is like a mighty tree to us** - an apple tree of the forest.

As we sit under the shade of his guidance and teaching we partake of his fruit which is sweet to our taste v3. The fruit of the Spirit forms in our character - love, joy, peace, patience, kindness, goodness, faithfulness, gentleness and self-control. These only appear as we keep in step with the Spirit Gal 5:22.

He has taken me to the banquet hall v4 We feed on his Word daily and are nourished by new revelation and wisdom through the Holy Spirit. We are satisfied with the words he speaks as we experience his love, provision and direction in all areas of life Ps 63:2-5; Mt 4:4.

His banner over me is love v4 He strengthens, protects and sustains us to be effective in service. We learn to walk under his royal standard v5-7.

Do not arouse or waken love until it so desires v7 This relationship only comes as we wait on him and spend time with him. Do nothing to disturb it!

***2:8-17 Arise and come with me* v10** He will call us to action. We are saved to serve - *just as the Son of Man did not come to be served but to serve and give his life as a ransom for many Mt 10:26-28*. We do not go alone – he will go with us and provide the increase for our work v8-13.

The clefts of the rock v14 We experience his presence on the way as we continue to abide in him - the joy of fellowship in action Jn 15:4. How precious is that place where we may stand on a rock, in all our circumstances knowing the security of his abiding presence and direction Ex 33:21-23.

The little foxes that ruin the vineyards v15 He will protect us from the interference of the evil one in our thoughts, lives and effectiveness in service.

My lover is mine and I am his v16 We give ourselves to him in undivided devotion as he has given himself to us and for us. *I no longer live, but Christ lives in me Gal 2:20.*

Lost Commitment

3:1-5 Fellowship can be broken - by sin, disobedience or neglecting our Quiet Times with the LORD v1. We may not recognize the loss due to gradual attraction of the world or our busyness 1Jn 2:15. *I looked for the one my heart loves - but did not find him v1* - suddenly we remember what we have lost. There is a strong connection between love and commitment, union and service, fellowship and commitment – as union wanes, love grows cold and service becomes less.
I will search for the one my heart loves v2. We must get up and search for that relationship again by returning to his Word and our times of devotion v2. He will return when we return and we must not let him go! v4,5; 2:7.

Recommitment

3:6-11 He is ever within reach He is ready to restore us to communion, waiting for us to seek him. When we are in fellowship we want others to know about him too v11, to see him as the Savior, King of kings and LORD of lords Rev 19:16.

4:1-7 We are beautiful to Jesus We must come to understand how much we mean to him. He loves us so much that he laid down his life for us 1Jn 4:10. His joy is in us Jn 15:11. There is no flaw in us because he cleansed us with his blood v7; 1Cor 6:11. Separation never comes from him.

4:8 Come with Me Because he has equipped us for service he calls us to come, not on our own, but with him v8. One of the great joys we experience is the fellowship we have with Jesus while in service Mt 28:20 - his joy is in us Jn 15:11. Whatever he calls us to we must do with all our heart for our devotion and love are delightful to him. We bear his message.
We must also remember that our service and even our devotion depend on him. We bring our 'loaves and fishes' to him and he provides the increase Mt 14:17,18. *Apart from me you can do nothing Jn 15:5.*

4:9,10 You have stolen my heart We must also understand that Jesus longs for us more than we could for him - our fellowship with him is not just for ourselves but for him - *as the Father has loved me so I have loved you - now remain in my love Jn 15:9;* 2Cor 8:9.

4:12-16 You are a garden locked up We are each like a garden with great potential, to produce much fruit - but we hold the key. We must unlock the garden, release the spring, telling others about him - ministering, feeding, encouraging, building up all those he leads across our path - leading them to share in our relationship with him v12-15. We want to rise up to bring joy to him because he enjoys the fruit of our service v16.

5:1 The LORD seeks communion with us because of his love for us. We must learn to seek him for his presence and joy rather than for our needs. **Daily devotion is for him as much as it is for us as he delights in us**! Sharing, hearing, speaking, meditating and waiting comes with practice in his presence Gal 5:25 - *blessed are those who have learned to acclaim you, who walk in the light of your presence, O LORD - they rejoice in your name all day long and exult in your righteousness Ps 89:15,16;* Eph 5:18-20.

Loss of Zeal

5:2-8 Sleep but the heart awake v2 We may enter the sleep of maturity. We have been enthusiastic in youth but grow slack with age. Our heart may be open to the LORD but it is easy to fall into slumber. We still believe but we fall away from serving, becoming lukewarm Rev 3:16. We may have neglected our Quiet Time, maybe lost motivation for our service or become too busy. Perhaps we are hurt by someone or become disappointed or dissatisfied. We may just settle in to the comfort, pleasures and activities or routine of the world. It may be that self-interest rises again. The devil would make us ineffective through the many attractions of worldly ways.

The Lord calls He knocks and pleads, but we do not act - the door is locked Rev 3:20. We are slow to respond. We become wearied by the cares, pressures or pleasures of the world v7; Mt 13:20-22. These things disqualify us from higher service. We rise too late with regret.

To avoid this situation we must be ever vigilant in our commitment to personal devotion and our response to his regular call to acts of service.

Rededication – two questions to ask -

5:9-16 Turn your eyes upon Jesus The benefit of close regular fellowship with other believers is seen in the inquiry *'how beautiful is your beloved?' v9*. This is a good question to ask of oneself. We need frequently to reflect on what Jesus means to us, what he has done for us and how much we have loved him v10-16. This will always spur us on to renewed devotion and fresh commitment. Our focus determines the direction and zeal of our interests Col 3:1-4.

This is also a good question to ask of others!

6:1-12 What is Jesus doing now? Fellowship with other believers can draw us back into service. This is another revealing question regarding commitment *'where is your lover now? v1.* He will always be in the garden about the Father's work v2; Jn 5:17. The LORD will respond to our recommitment when it is accompanied by a willing heart, when we give him our undivided devotion again v3,4. Though he is a King and we of lowly stock we have been chosen by him from among all people, before the foundation of the world, each of us his individual unique selection v9; Eph 1:4. He will have new tasks for us in the new growth, amongst the buds and blooms - with the salvation of the unsaved, discipling and building the believers v11,12; Col 1:28,29.

6:13 The call of the world Friends and acquaintances may also call us back from our service into the world. Our commitment may make them uncomfortable. We may even be discouraged by those who do not recognize our call. The leading of the LORD will keep us consistent 1Sam 29:9.

Mission for Life

7:1-10 Now I belong to Jesus Once again we will be a delight to the LORD and our desire is to please him. There is no more of self. We belong to him in unbroken communion and devoted service and his desire is for us!

7:10-13 To see if the vines have budded We go to him and find pleasure with him in the field, regardless of the effort v11. We have pleasure with him in viewing together the fruits of our labor v12,13.

One of the greatest joys is in being used by the LORD to bring someone to commitment - this is holy ground – to see the Holy Spirit at work in the person. We know it is only possible through our yielding to him and our willingness to be used by him.

8:1-5 We are Family For all the joy of romantic love there is a desire in the heart for family relationship. We have been born again into the family of God – we are children of the Father, sons and co-heirs with Christ Rom 8:17. We are one with the Trinity - Father, Son and Holy Spirit! Jn 17:20-23.

We may therefore lean on him completely and in every situation v5.

8:6,7 The Holy Spirit is the seal that secures our love for Jesus, a love that is ardent, that burns like a blazing fire in us and produces a mighty flame Jer 20:9. What can separate us from his love in us? Rom 8:35.

8:8,9 Making Disciples A joy of discipleship is to be involved in discipling another – to bring them into your relationship with Jesus. To share your Quite Time with them and teach them to exercise the spiritual disciplines and see them grow to love him too. As we have learned, so we seek to encourage others so that in turn they may teach others 2Tim 2:2.

8:10-13 My vineyard is mine to give v12 Our life is like a vineyard, given to us by God. We may grow fruit for self, for this life or for eternal life – it is ours to choose – ours to give. May we be faithful tenants Mt 21:33.

8:14 **The Wedding of the Lamb** The union we experience with Jesus in life is but a foretaste of eternal life. May we make ourselves ready to be partakers with the Groom Rev 19:7.

BOOKS OF THE BIBLE
[39 + 27 = 66]

BOOKS OF THE OLD TESTAMENT
[39]

	HISTORY (17)	POETRY (5)	PROPHECY (17)	
LAW (5)	Genesis	Job	Isaiah	**MAJOR (5)**
Pentateuch	Exodus	Psalms	Jeremiah	
Books of Moses	Leviticus	Proverbs	Lamentations	
	Numbers	Ecclesiastes	Ezekiel	
	Deuteronomy	Solomon	Daniel	
HISTORY (12)	Joshua		Hosea	**MINOR (12)**
of Israel	Judges		Joel	
	Ruth		Amos	
	1 Samuel		Obadiah	
	2 Samuel		Jonah	
	1 Kings		Micah	
	2 Kings		Nahum	
	1 Chronicles		Habakkuk	
	2 Chronicles		Zephaniah	
	Ezra	Post Exile	Haggai	
	Nehemiah		Zechariah	
	Esther		Malachi	

BOOKS OF THE NEW TESTAMENT
[27]

	HISTORY (5)	LETTERS OF PAUL (13)	GENERAL LETTERS (9)	
GOSPELS (4)	Matthew	Romans	Hebrews	Unknown
	Mark	1 Corinthians	James	Other
	Luke	2 Corinthians	1 Peter	Apostles (7)
	John	Glatians	2 Peter	
Early Church (1)	Acts	Ephesians	1 John	
Luke		Philippians	2 John	
		Colossians	3 John	
		1 Thessalonians	Jude	
		2 Thessalonians	Revelation	John
		1 Timothy		
		2 Timothy		
		Titus		
		Philemon		

The Layman's Commentary Series contains the following -